BROWNIES
to die for!

*Cut a brownie into a unique shape, plate it with a cream sauce,
decorate it with an edible flower, and transform a comfort-food
dessert from yum to wow, in this delicious Glazed Brownie Triangle.*

BROWNIES
to die for!

BEV SHAFFER

PELICAN PUBLISHING COMPANY
GRETNA 2006

The word "Pelican" and the depiction of a pelican are trademarks
of Pelican Publishing Company, Inc., and are registered in the
U.S. Patent and Trademark Office.

Library of Congress Cataloging-in-Publication Data

Shaffer, Bev, 1951-
  Brownies to die for! / Bev Shaffer.
        p. cm.
  Includes bibliographical references and index.
  ISBN-13: 978-1-58980-382-4 (hardcover : alk. paper)
  1. Brownies (Cookery) I. Title.
  TX771.S33 2006
  641.8'653—dc22

                                                2005030575

Photographs and food styling by John Shaffer

Printed in Singapore
Published by Pelican Publishing Company, Inc.
1000 Burmaster Street, Gretna, Louisiana 70053

Special thanks to all my taste testers who contributed their waistlines to this book.

Thanks to my friend, Vickie, for her proofreading skills and ever-so-tactful explanations of what she liked and didn't like about my writing style.

Thanks to my husband, dear friend, and unwavering supporter, John . . . for baking brownies when I simply didn't have the time (hey, somebody's got to do it!); for reading and reworking recipes with me; for taking the mouth-watering photographs you see in this cookbook that simply say "bake me"; for egging me on a long, long time ago by saying, "don't be discouraged if the answer is no"; and, most of all, just for being himself!

I'd also like to dedicate this book to the National Hockey League. As a longtime fan (as in fanatical), I was desperate for a hockey game during their strike and went to an American Hockey League game. I broke my finger on my right hand at the game—and (being right handed, of course) typed, edited, and retyped this entire manuscript with the finger splinted, two surgeries, three pins, and much agony. Just one season of no hockey, and see what an out-of-practice hockey fan has to go through?!

And, yes, Ray—there are still some Chocolate-Ganache-Topped Brownies left in the freezer . . . I think!

CONTENTS

A helping hand and a Chocolate-Ganache-Topped Brownie are welcome additions to any kitchen!

BROWNIE BITES

I remember my first taste of a brownie as though it were yesterday. A grade-school friend's mom was of Swiss descent, and my friend invited me into her kitchen one day to taste this chocolaty, cakelike concoction that her mom called a "brownie square." It was heavenly . . . moist, dense, and—oh! that flavor of chocolate was sublime! I rushed home to tell my mom about it, hoping that she'd dedicate every waking minute to the pursuit of baking me the perfect "brownie square." "Chocolate is not something I bake with, but I'd be happy to make you some nut roll," my mom countered, not even looking up from making her stuffed cabbage.

I was crushed!—but determined to use my childish ways to convince my mom that somewhere in her Hungarian ancestry her relatives, too, had made "brownie squares" and the recipe had simply been lost. Many nut rolls later, I filed the taste of those "brownie squares" in the back of my mind. . . .

Since then, I've become a brownie snob. It's not necessarily something I talk about in public. Lots of people are perfectly satisfied with wasting their calories on something they can concoct out of a box mix (add egg, water, oil, and—like magic!—brownies!). Not me. I want deep, dense, chocolate brownies . . . slightly underbaked so they melt on the tongue, and you can close your eyes when you eat them. The kind of brownies that I can add toasted walnuts or pecans to, chunks of semisweet chocolate to . . . and once they're baked and I take a bite, they're crunchy with just a hint of cake that enrobes the nuts and chocolate pieces.

I've devoted hours and hours of baking and playing-in-the-kitchen time to creating and perfecting this assortment of brownie recipes. They're my creations (or those of friends—chefs, bakers, culinary students), all with my fine-tuning and reworking. I've taught them in cooking classes, written about them in food columns, demonstrated them on television, and moaned over them on radio. I even have the thighs to prove it!

If I ever wound up in court I'd have my lawyer tell the judge, "Your honor, this woman wants only the basics—shelter, clothing, transportation, and the ability to buy the very best chocolate whenever the [need] urge strikes her" (which would be often!).

If I was sitting across from someone at a restaurant, and they were pouring their heart out to me but hadn't touched their extravagant brownie dessert, I'd be distracted! "Oh that's terrible," I'd say. "Are you going to finish your dessert?"

I know this all sounds beyond reason, but it's true. I love brownies. The ingredients need to be basic and the very best—unsalted butter, unbleached all-purpose flour, toasted nuts. I add a layer of this and a topping of that and use chocolate with the highest cocoa-butter content and the least amount of sweetness. Then I can bake them, cut them, savor them, and say, *"Wow!"*

Research tells us that twelve out of every ten people love chocolate. Based on this statistic, brownies are the perfect dessert to lure anyone into an agreeable trance any day. Brownies are sexy, not stuffy. They're complex in flavor and texture but not complicated to make and bake.

Chocolate varieties abound, so I've included in my "Chocolate Info" chapter a little Chocolate 101, complete with chocolate melting tips, to get you started if you're not (yet) a passionate baker. I love the better-quality chocolates that are generous in cocoa butter and provide the richest mouth feel. (My favorites are: Callebaut, from Belgium, for everything from unsweetened to bitter- or semisweet, milk, and white chocolate; Valrhona, from France, for bittersweet or milk, but I especially love their white chocolate and their unsweetened cocoa powder; Scharffen Berger, from California, for their unsweetened, semisweet, and bittersweet chocolate. For chocolate chips, I prefer either Guittard, Callebaut, or Ghirardelli. Any of these makes a superb brownie.) But I'm always trying the newest artisan chocolate on the market—varieties and labels abound. This is the perfect excuse to buy various types of chocolate and taste for quality and degrees of sweetness (or lack thereof)!

So let's not delay the choc-euphoria any longer. Heat the oven, and get out the mixing bowls and whisk. Ready, set, bake—it's brownie time!

BROWNIES
to die for!

A HISTORY OF BROWNIES

Was it a failed chocolate cake or a purposely concocted idea? Like the ingredients in your favorite bakery's decadent chocolate desserts, mystery and intrigue surround the birth of brownies!

Some attribute the first brownie to Mildred Brown Schrumpf. Mildred (affectionately known as "Brownie") was a Maine home economist, nutritionist, newspaper columnist, food judge, author, and, of course, cook. Were brownies her invention?

Others assert that the American favorite was first mentioned in an 1897 Sears-Roebuck catalog, in a reference to mail-order chocolate candies named after cartoon elves created in a book series that began with *The Brownies: Their Book*.

Most often, however, sources tempt your brownie curiosity and quiz-show skills by telling you that the earliest recipes appear in *The Boston Cooking School Cookbook*, published in 1906.

Let's follow the crumb trail, however, back to Mildred Brown Schrumpf and the state of Maine. A note in *Betty Crocker's Baking Classics*, circa 1979, claims that Bangor Brownies (as in Bangor, Maine) are probably the original chocolate brownies. According to this classic cookbook, legend has it that a Maine housewife was baking a chocolate cake and it fell (not on the floor, but deflated!). Instead of discarding it, this frugal cook cut the collapsed cake into bars and served it—to nothing short of rave reviews. (It's an intriguing baking myth—but a little hard to swallow. How did she know how to make that collapsed cake again?!)

Whatever the true origins, brownies didn't become popular until the 1920s, coinciding with the mass production, availability, and affordability of chocolate.

And there's no stopping our brownie baking and creativity now!

BAKING BASICS

Many of you probably *did not* grow up baking and cooking in the kitchen with your mom or dad. I'm aware of this from teaching Basic Baking and Basic Cookery classes. This chapter is for you—tips that will help ensure success and help you become enthusiastic about the art and pleasure of scratch baking.

I know, I know—time is short. So is life! Don't waste it on eating poor-quality brownies.

If you keep a few basics in your pantry, you'll have what it takes to whip up brownies in no time flat. And if you have kids, invite them into the kitchen with you to share in the fun, the mess, the measuring, the scooping, the baking, and the cleanup—all with the final reward of great taste and time well spent! No kids? Share the fun with friends or a spouse.

Are you an experienced baker? It's always good to review, if for nothing more than the pleasure of saying, "Yeah, I know that!"

I'm a real believer in *mise en place*—a French term that refers to having all ingredients necessary for baking or cooking prepared (i.e., chopped or toasted) and ready to combine (i.e., measured) up to the point of baking or cooking. I emphasize and reemphasize this to all my students. All things measured and ready eliminates surprises such as not enough sugar, only one egg, no buttermilk, etc., and forces you to reread the recipe instructions when ready to bake or cook.

LOTS OF MY RECIPES SAY . . .

Nuts, toasted: Toast pecans, walnuts, almonds, and other nuts in a dry skillet over low heat until fragrant, watching carefully so they don't burn. (This process only takes a few minutes.) Yes, you could also do this in a 325-degree or higher oven on a cookie sheet, but I find a dry skillet so much more convenient.

Do not overbake: Why? Brownies become dry and hard when overbaked. Underset your timer, be sure your oven temperature is accurate, and test your brownies for doneness. A brownie that's just right will be moist and flavorful. So bake those brownies, as it states, "until a cake tester or toothpick inserted . . . comes out with a few moist crumbs attached."

Softened to room temperature: This *does not* mean melted. Take your butter or cream cheese or whatever the recipe calls for out of the refrigerator 30 minutes before using, to soften. Adding melted ingredients to a Brownie Base will cause textural changes in the final product.

Divided: When you're getting your ingredients ready (remember *mise en place!*), it's much easier to know in advance that you need to divide up the butter (and cut it while it's cold) for separate uses in the same recipe, or divide up the chocolate (and weigh it in appropriate batches while the scale is out).

Unsalted butter: I use unsalted butter because it provides a better mouth feel (and overall flavor), you can control the amount of salt in a recipe (all manufacturers of salted butter have a different standard), and it lets the cows know I'm a purist!

MY WRITING STYLE

I've tried to anticipate your questions (this comes from years of culinary teaching) and keep things simple. Even recipes with many steps are written in an easy-to-understand manner. I like to throw in a sarcastic/humorous remark now and again . . . in case you're forgetting to enjoy the experience and smile!

THINGS YOU NEED TO KNOW

Measure ingredients accurately and follow instructions carefully. Baking offers less room for interpretation than do other forms of cooking.

Use a good thermometer to check the oven temperature. Ovens are often inaccurately calibrated, which accounts for many baking problems.

Use an accurate kitchen scale. Buy one that is very accurate and weighs in ounces and grams and, if possible, goes up to one pound. Be sure the ounce and gram marks are easy to read. Lots of recipes call for one ounce of this and that. Weighing ingredients should not require a magnifying glass!

Use the pan size called for unless you are an experienced baker and know how to make the necessary adjustments. (My husband, John, does this for me—his degree is in math!)

Store pecans, walnuts, almonds, and other nuts in the refrigerator and freezer to prevent them from going rancid. Toast when using to add that crunch again.

Separate egg whites and yolks carefully, since a speck of fatty yolk in the whites will prevent them from whipping to maximum volume. (The best way to separate an egg is to carefully pour the egg into your clean hand and let the white run through your fingers.) Eggs separate best when chilled but whip best at room temperature.

Measure flour by spooning it into a dry measuring cup and leveling it off with a knife. Don't pack it down.

To line a pan with foil the easy way, turn the pan upside down on the counter. Center a piece of foil (larger than the pan) over the pan. Fold the edges of the foil down over the four sides of the pan, folding the corners neatly as though wrapping a package. Slip the foil off the pan. Turn the pan right side up and press the foil (*gently*) into the pan, smoothing it across the bottom, into the corners, and up the sides.

To grease a pan, use a paper towel, pastry brush, waxed paper, or your clean fingers and lightly coat the inside bottom and sides of the pan with softened butter or shortening. I prefer these two choices to sprays. You'll get more even results and no aftertaste.

Make your own pure vanilla extract! Buy a 375-milliliter bottle of 80 proof, moderately priced vodka (such as Smirnoff). Cut two vanilla beans in half crosswise (resulting in four pieces) and place all four pieces into the bottle of vodka. Label and let steep in a cool place (out of direct light) for over four weeks or until the vanilla smells right. You will see little flecks of vanilla seeds floating in the vodka. Do not be alarmed; this is a great thing! Also, you will notice that your "vanilla" does not become excessively dark. That's because there is no coloring in it. It's pure and natural. Leave the beans in the bottle until you use up all the liquid. My preference for type of vanilla bean is Madagascar Bourbon beans, for maximum flavor. Homemade extract makes a wonderful gift for someone who loves to bake.

MEASURING

Baking is both an art and a science. To satisfy the scientific part, you must be accurate and consistent when measuring ingredients. Not all ingredients are measured the same way.

Yes, Virginia, there *is* a difference between dry and liquid measuring cups!

A dry measuring cup is a straight-sided, graduated cup with a handle attached at the top lip. The most common sizes are $\frac{1}{4}$, $\frac{1}{3}$, $\frac{1}{2}$, 1, and 2 cups. They are used to measure a standard amount of dry ingredients (such as flour, sugar, brown sugar, etc.).

Granulated or confectioners' sugar should be spooned into a dry measuring cup and leveled off. Brown sugar, on the other hand, should be pressed firmly into a dry measure so it holds the shape of the cup when it is turned out (this is referred to as "firmly packed").

Proper measuring of flour is critical. Too much flour can cause baked goods to turn out dry. To measure flour, stir it in the bag or container to lighten it. Gently spoon flour into a dry measuring cup or a measuring spoon. Level it off at the top with a straight-edged utensil.

A liquid measuring cup is clear, hard plastic or glass with a lip for pouring. The cup is usually a pint or quart measuring tool marked with lines to measure liquid ingredients. The lines will mark ounces, milliliters, and $\frac{1}{8}$, $\frac{1}{4}$, $\frac{1}{3}$, $\frac{1}{2}$, $\frac{2}{3}$, $\frac{3}{4}$, and 1 cup or more. Liquid ingredients should be measured in this cup, with the cup placed on a flat, level surface for accuracy.

When liquid is measured in a measuring spoon, fill the spoon to the top but don't let it spill over. Don't pour liquid ingredients over the other ingredients, in case you spill!

Should you chop before or after you measure? Simply check the way the ingredient is listed. For example, if it says *3 tbsp. walnuts, coarsely chopped,* the action is after the amount, so measure—then chop. If, however, it says *3 tbsp. coarsely chopped walnuts,* the action is before the amount, so (you guessed it) chop—then measure.

The same is true with sifting. For example, if it says *1½ cups confectioners' sugar, sifted,* the action is after the amount, so measure—then sift.

Butter is measured in its solid (stick) form. One stick of butter is equal to 8 tbsp. (½ cup); two sticks equal 16 tbsp. (1 cup). One pound of butter is equal to 32 tbsp. (2 cups). Butter sticks are usually wrapped in paper with preprinted graduated tablespoon markings.

WHAT DOES IT MEAN?

Here are explanations of terms and ingredients if you've never baked before. (I've always taught my students that no question is too basic if you don't know the answer.) Refer to my chapter "Ingredient Preferences and Sources" to find a few of my choices.

All-purpose flour: Wheat flour milled from hard wheat or a blend of soft and hard wheat. May be used in a variety of baked goods and pasta making.

All-purpose flour, unbleached: Flour that is bleached naturally as it ages; no maturing agents are used in the milling process.

Arrowroot: The starchy product of the tropical tuber of the same name, the roots of which are dried and ground into a very fine powder. Used as a thickening agent, it is absolutely tasteless and becomes clear when cooked.

Bakeware: Made in a range of materials: aluminum, tin, stainless steel, black steel, glass, and pottery. Both the material and finish affect the final product. Shiny bakeware reflects heat, slowing the browning process. On the other hand, dark and dull-finish bakeware absorbs more heat, increasing the amount of browning.

Baking powder: A leavening agent containing both baking soda and one or two acids—citric or tartaric. Double acting is used in home kitchens because it has two types of acid—one reacts when liquids are added in the bowl and the other reacts when it becomes hot during baking. Don't know if the baking powder that's been in your cupboard forever is still good? Test for strength by mixing 1 tsp. baking powder with ¼ cup very hot water. The mixture should bubble furiously if the powder is all right.

Baking soda (bicarbonate of soda): Creates carbon dioxide when mixed in a batter with liquid and acidic ingredients (such as sour milk or buttermilk, lemon or orange juice, vinegar, honey, or chocolate). The reaction begins as soon as the liquids are added to the dry ingredients in the bowl.

Batter: A mixture usually made with flour and a liquid. Batters vary in consistency from thin enough to pour to thick enough to drop from a spoon.

Beat: Make a smooth mixture by whipping or stirring with a wire whisk, spoon, old-fashioned egg beater, or electric mixer.

Blend: Mix two or more ingredients together with a spoon, wire whisk, electric mixer, blender, or food processor.

Bloom: Pale, grayish streaks or blotches on the surface of chocolate indicating the cocoa butter has separated from the chocolate. This means the chocolate was stored in too warm an environment, but it can still be used. (Store chocolate, well wrapped, in a cool, dry place away from direct sunlight and heat.)

Butter: Produced by churning cream into a semisolid form. By the U.S. standard definition, it is 80 percent milk fat, with the remaining 20 percent consisting of water and milk solids. Butter may be salted or unsalted (sweet) and is valued by most bakers for its irreplaceable flavor and ability to create crispness and tenderness.

Cake flour: Fine-textured, silky flour milled from soft wheat. Cake flour has a low-protein content for making cakes, cookies, and pastries with a soft crumb. It should always be sifted before using.

Caramelize: Heat and stir sugar until it melts and turns a golden brown.

Combine: Mix together.

Confectioners' sugar or powdered sugar: A granulated sugar that has been crushed into a fine powder. A small amount (about 3 percent) of cornstarch is added to some brands to prevent clumping.

Cooling rack: A rectangular grid of thick wire with "feet" that raise it above the countertop. Used to cool cakes, cookies, brownies, and other baked goods when they come out of the oven, allowing air to circulate around the pan (top and bottom) to prevent moisture from forming and making the baked goods soggy.

Cream: Use a wire whisk, electric mixer, or large spoon to mix fats (butter or other shortening) and sugars together until light and smooth in appearance.

Drizzle: To pour a liquid (such as a glaze) in a random pattern in a thin stream over food.

Electric mixer: A machine to make life easier in the kitchen. Handheld electric mixers are perfect for light jobs (like whipping cream); stand electric mixers (such as Kitchen Aid) are perfect for heavy-duty jobs and long mixing periods. They also work perfectly for whipping cream.

Food processor: A machine that can blend, chop and puree, slice and shred, mix batters, and blend pastry.

Framboise: Liqueur with a raspberry flavor. (The word is French for raspberry.)

Frost: Apply a sweet topping to a brownie, cake, or cookie. The topping is soft enough to spread but stiff enough to hold its shape.

Ganache: A rich chocolate icing usually made with bittersweet chocolate and heavy (whipping) cream. Ganache, once made and cooled to lukewarm, is poured over a brownie, cake, or torte for a satiny, glossy finish.

Glaze: A thin, glossy coating on a food.

Grand Marnier: French liqueur with a Cognac base, flavored with bitter orange peel.

Grease: Coat a baking pan or skillet with a thin layer of fat or oil.

Instant espresso powder: Available at most supermarkets, the intense flavor of this quick-dissolving powder is perfect for adding a coffee kick to brownies. I prefer to buy imported Italian brands.

Insulated baking pans: Metal bakeware constructed of two layers separated by an insulating cushion of air. Benefits include more even baking with less bottom-crust browning.

Jellyroll pan: A rectangular baking pan that features a 1" edge and is most commonly 13x18" or 15½ x 10½" in size.

Kirsch: Liqueur with a cherry flavor. (The word is German for cherry.)

Marble: Gently swirl one food into another; usually done with light and dark batters for brownies or cakes.

Mix: Stir, usually with a spoon or spatula, until the ingredients are well combined (individual ingredients can no longer be seen or identified).

Pipe: Force a semisoft food, such as frosting or whipped cream, through a pastry bag to decorate.

Sauté pan: A wide pan with straight or minimally curved sides; similar in looks (except the sides are higher) to a frying pan.

Sift: Put one or several dry ingredients through a sifter or sieve to remove lumps and make batter smoother.

Spread: Distribute an ingredient in a thin layer over the surface of another item.

Springform pan: A cake pan whose bottom and sides are removed from the baked cake by means of a spring or hinge, so there is no need to invert the cake.

Sprinkle: Scatter bits of topping over a surface (e.g., "sprinkle nuts atop frosting").

Stir: Use a spoon to mix ingredients with a circular motion.

Superfine sugar: Also known as castor sugar, a more finely granulated sugar than traditional granulated cane sugar.

Vanilla powder: The whole dried vanilla bean ground until powdery. Vanilla powder's flavor doesn't evaporate as readily as vanilla extract, so it's especially suited for anything heated (baked goods, puddings, custards, and more).

Whip: Beat a mixture lightly with an electric mixer, wire whisk, or old-fashioned egg beater to incorporate air and increase volume.

Whisk: Traditionally, a utensil made of a group of looped wires held together by a long handle. When you whisk ingredients, you use this utensil to lighten the ingredients and incorporate air.

Zest: The thin, colorful outer skin of citrus fruit removed with a zester, vegetable peeler, paring knife, or, my favorite, a Microplane zester/grater. The aromatic, flavorful pieces are used to enhance baked goods. Most typically, zests used are from fresh oranges and lemons. The zest never includes the white pith underneath, which is bitter.

Some basic baking knowledge, the right ingredients and tools—like a whisk—and you have brownies!

CHOCOLATE INFO

Pay attention—this is the stuff they ask you on quiz shows!

The cocoa tree is grown in hot, rainy climates in an area known as the "cocoa belt." The most prolific of the cocoa-producing nations are Madagascar, Venezuela, Indonesia, Ecuador, Grenada, and a number of countries in the equatorial regions of Africa.

Four primary groupings of cocoa beans make up the world's chocolate production:

Criollo accounts for 1 percent of the world's cocoa production. It is the most sought after of all cocoa beans and is the most difficult to grow. Its low acid level and pleasing aroma produce a smooth, full-flavored chocolate.

Trinitario accounts for 5 percent of the world's cocoa production. It is easily cultivated and noted for its fine aromatic flavor.

Nacional accounts for 2 percent of the world's cocoa production. It is noted for its sweetness and aromatic flavor.

Forastero accounts for 92 percent of the world's cocoa production. It is much easier to cultivate than the other beans, producing a higher yield at a lower cost. This bean has a more astringent taste.

If you paid attention to math in school, it'll be very clear that premium cocoa beans account for only 8 percent of the world's total cocoa production. Chocolates formulated from this small harvest are the pride of artisan producers.

Companies that produce this kind of chocolate use their own process for blending, roasting, and grinding—a process known as conching (combining the cocoa paste with cocoa butter at high temperatures while exposing the mixture to a blast of fresh air). Why? Chemical changes that take place during conching remove any musty or sour taste, develop the chocolate's delicate flavor, and give it the "snap" characteristic of excellent chocolate. These producers also use cane sugar, pure vanilla, cocoa solids, and cocoa butter instead of the less expensive beet sugar, vanillin, and waxy stabilizers found in many mainstream chocolates.

Buy quality chocolates (see some of my choices in "Ingredient Preferences and Sources"). You'll be rewarded with exceptional taste.

THE LANGUAGE OF CHOCOLATE

Cacao: The seed of a tropical evergreen tree used in making chocolate, cocoa, and cocoa butter.

Cocoa beans: The source of all cocoa and chocolate products, cocoa beans are found in the pods of the cocoa tree.

Chocolate liquor: This base of all chocolate and cocoa is produced by grinding the cocoa beans, resulting in a rich, dark-brown, liquid mass.

Cocoa butter: This is the natural fat of the cocoa bean, which is pressed from the chocolate liquor when making cocoa powder. Look for a high cocoa content when shopping—50 to 75 percent cocoa solids are usually a good sign.

Bittersweet, semisweet, and sweet chocolate: Each is prepared by blending chocolate liquor with varying amounts of sweeteners and cocoa butter. Sweet chocolate contains at least 15 percent chocolate liquor, while semisweet and bittersweet contain at least 35 percent.

Milk chocolate: America's favorite form, milk chocolate is made by adding cocoa butter, milk, sweeteners, and flavorings to chocolate liquor.

White chocolate: According to the FDA, this is really not a chocolate at all because it does not contain chocolate liquor. It is a blend of sugar, cocoa butter, dry milk solids, flavorings such as vanilla, and emulsifiers. Be sure the words "cocoa butter" are listed in the ingredients; otherwise you're simply buying candy coating made with flavorings and fats. Real white chocolate comes in shades of ivory, while other products normally called white "confections" are usually bright white.

Unsweetened chocolate: 99 percent cacao (unlike bittersweet, which contains some sugar). It contains about 50 percent cocoa butter. Unsweetened chocolate allows you to make desserts with a more intense chocolate flavor, controlling the degree of sweetness.

Cocoa powder: The soft brown powder obtained after most of the cocoa butter has been removed from chocolate liquor.

CUTTING CHOCOLATE

Mark the chocolate at the place you want to cut with the blade of a sharp, hard steel knife. Gently press down, rocking the knife back and forth until the piece splits off.

For easy melting, cut the chocolate into small pieces (e.g., referred to in my recipes as *coarsely chopped*) with a sharp knife as above, an ice pick, or a chocolate chopper. Cut on a heavy cutting board.

MELTING CHOCOLATE

Chocolate is best *melted slowly* and by *gentle heat*.

In the top of a double boiler over hot, not boiling, water (to avoid any rising steam), melt chocolate, stirring often and carefully monitoring heat, since chocolate scorches easily. The bowl and spoon or heatproof spatula should be absolutely dry. A drop of moisture will cause the chocolate to thicken.

Chocolate as an art form. Actually, it's simply the very best chocolate waiting to be melted in a double boiler.

Chocolate that is overheated may scorch, lose flavor, and turn coarse and grainy.

In many of my recipes I melt chocolate and butter in a saucepan directly over *low heat,* stirring often. As long as you're diligent about watching the mixture carefully and stirring often, this works well. Remember, too high a heat will scorch the mixture and—voila!—good ingredients go to waste.

If you'd rather melt chocolate in a microwave oven, do so with caution, stirring frequently and melting on nothing more than medium power. Stir melting chocolate after it has just begun to liquefy.

Because of the sensitivity of milk solids to heat, milk and white chocolate should be stirred almost constantly. Dark chocolate need only be stirred frequently during melting.

Note: Cool melted chocolate to room temperature before adding to brownie batters. Adding hot melted chocolate will cause a textural change.

The best news of all is that chocolate contains "healthy" antioxidants. Research on antioxidants is still in its infancy, but cocoa powder and dark chocolate ranked highest in chocolate products. (So help a researcher and eat a piece of plain dark chocolate today.)

CLASSIC BROWNIES: NEW AND OLD FAVORITES

Your Momma's Buttermilk Brownie with my momma!

Plain and Simple Fudgy Brownies

This is the recipe we make at home again and again when we want to get that quick but oh-so-delicious brownie fix!

BROWNIE BASE

4 oz. unsweetened chocolate, coarsely
   chopped
²⁄₃ cup unsalted butter
2 cups granulated sugar
4 large eggs, lightly beaten
1 tsp. pure vanilla extract
1¼ cups unbleached, all-purpose flour
1 tsp. baking powder
1 tsp. salt
1 cup chopped walnuts or pecans, lightly
   toasted

Heat oven to 350 degrees. Lightly grease a 13x9" baking pan.

For the Brownie Base: Melt the chocolate and butter in a medium saucepan over low heat, stirring to blend. Remove pan from heat and whisk in sugar, eggs, and vanilla.

Stir in flour, baking powder, salt, and nuts. Spread into prepared pan. Bake for 25 minutes or until the brownies *just* begin to pull away from the sides of the pan. Brownies will be dry if overbaked! Cool pan slightly (or just until the brownies will no longer burn the roof of your mouth!). Cut into bars. Makes about 2 dozen.

BEV'S BITE —————

Walnuts and pecans should be stored in the refrigerator or freezer to prevent them from becoming rancid. To crisp up their taste again, lightly toast them before using. The easiest way to do this is to spread them in a large, dry skillet and toast them on the burner over low/medium heat until fragrant, stirring often to prevent burning. This takes several minutes. Cool completely before using in a recipe.

What could be better than a brownie and a glass of milk? Two brownies and a glass of milk!

Chocolate Brownies

Don't let the plain name fool you. The flavor is anything but plain! Vary the nuts (or use several types in the same brownie) for something different.

BROWNIE BASE
1½ cups unsalted butter
1½ cups unsweetened cocoa powder, sifted
6 large eggs, lightly beaten
3 cups superfine sugar
¼ cup granulated sugar
1⅔ cups unbleached, all-purpose flour
1½ tsp. pure vanilla extract
1 cup coarsely chopped pecans, toasted

Heat oven to 350 degrees. Line an 8x12" baking pan.

For the Brownie Base: Melt the butter in a large saucepan over low heat. Whisk in the cocoa powder, stirring until blended. Whisk the eggs, sugars, flour, and vanilla in a large bowl, blending gently until smooth. Stir in the cocoa/butter mixture and nuts.

Spread into prepared pan. Bake for 40 minutes or until a cake tester or toothpick inserted near the center comes out with a few moist crumbs attached. Brownies will be dry if overbaked! Cool pan completely on a wire rack. Cut into squares. Makes about 2 dozen.

Fudge Brownies

Brown sugar is the star in these rich, chocolaty, cakelike brownies. This very simple, one-saucepan recipe yields delicious results!

BROWNIE BASE
½ cup unsalted butter
3 oz. unsweetened chocolate, coarsely chopped
1 cup firmly packed light brown sugar
½ tsp. pure vanilla extract
2 large eggs, lightly beaten
½ cup unbleached, all-purpose flour
¼ cup mini semisweet chocolate chips

Heat oven to 350 degrees. Lightly grease an 8" square pan.

For the Brownie Base: Melt the butter and chocolate in a large saucepan over low heat until mixture is melted and smooth. Remove from heat. Cool slightly.

In a medium bowl with an electric mixer, beat sugar and vanilla on low speed just until combined. Beat in cooled butter/chocolate mixture on low speed until blended.

Add eggs, beating well. Beat in flour on medium-low speed until batter is smooth. Gently stir in chips. Spread into prepared pan. Bake for 25 minutes or until a cake tester or toothpick inserted near the center comes out with a few moist crumbs attached. Cool pan completely on a wire rack. Cut into squares. Makes about 1 dozen.

Brownies for a Crowd

This big batch of fudgy, frosted brownies is perfect when just a few won't do! They're perfect to go along with you to a picnic or family reunion or to share with friends.

BROWNIE BASE

2 oz. unsweetened chocolate, coarsely chopped
2 oz. bittersweet chocolate, coarsely chopped
1 cup unsalted butter, softened to room temperature
2 cups granulated sugar
½ cup sour cream (yes, you could use low fat—but what's the point?!)
4 large eggs, lightly beaten
2 tsp. pure vanilla extract
1¾ cups unbleached, all-purpose flour
¼ tsp. salt

CHOCOLATE FROSTING

4 oz. semisweet chocolate, coarsely chopped
2 oz. milk chocolate, coarsely chopped
2 tbsp. unsalted butter, softened to room temperature
1½ cups confectioners' sugar, sifted
½ tsp. pure vanilla extract
3 tbsp. or more heavy (whipping) cream or half-and-half

BEV'S BITE
Need more brownies for your crowd? Try Your Momma's Buttermilk Brownies (see index).

Heat oven to 350 degrees. Lightly grease a 15x10x1" baking pan.

For the Brownie Base: Combine the chocolates in a double boiler set over simmering water. Stir often, over low heat, until mixture is melted and smooth.

Remove top of double boiler from heat, and carefully wipe bottom (so none of the moisture steams up into the chocolate mixture). Whisk in butter to blend. Whisk in sugar until well combined.

With a large spoon, add sour cream, eggs, and vanilla; mix well. Gently add in flour and salt just until mixture is combined. Spread into prepared pan. Bake for 20 to 25 minutes or until a cake tester or toothpick inserted near the center comes out with a few moist crumbs attached. Brownies will be dry if overbaked! Cool pan completely on a wire rack.

For the Chocolate Frosting: Melt chocolates in a double boiler set over simmering water. Stir often, over low heat, until mixture is melted and smooth.

Remove top of double boiler from heat, and carefully wipe bottom (so none of the moisture steams up into the chocolate mixture). Whisk in butter, sugar, vanilla, and enough cream for a smooth spreadable frosting. Frost cooled brownies. Cut into bars. Makes about 4 dozen.

Brownies Smothered with Chocolate Frosting

Unsweetened cocoa powder stars in this chocolaty, frosty brownie! This is a very sweet brownie with a rich chocolate frosting that you simply must smother on (and, of course, lick your fingers after eating a square!).

BROWNIE BASE
1½ cups unsalted butter
1 cup unsweetened cocoa powder, sifted
2¼ cups granulated sugar
¼ cup firmly packed light brown sugar
6 large eggs, lightly beaten
1½ cups unbleached, all-purpose flour
1½ tsp. pure vanilla extract
¼ tsp. salt
1 cup coarsely chopped pecans, toasted

CHOCOLATE FROSTING
2 oz. bittersweet chocolate, coarsely chopped
¼ cup unsalted butter, softened to room temperature
1½ cups confectioners' sugar, sifted
3 tbsp. or more milk, whole or 2 percent
½ tsp. pure vanilla extract

Heat oven to 350 degrees. Lightly grease a 13x9" baking pan.

For the Brownie Base: Melt the butter in a medium saucepan over low heat. Whisk in the cocoa until smooth; cool slightly. Stir the sugars into cocoa mixture until combined. Whisk in eggs, blending well. Whisk in the flour, vanilla, and salt until blended. Gently stir in pecan pieces. Spread into prepared pan.

Bake for 45 minutes or until a cake tester or toothpick inserted in the center comes out with a few moist crumbs attached. Cool pan completely on a wire rack.

For the Chocolate Frosting: Melt the chocolate and butter in a medium saucepan over low heat, stirring until smooth and blended. With an electric mixer, beat in sugar, milk, and vanilla on low speed to blend, then increase speed to medium high and beat until frosting is smooth and spreadable.

Frost cooled brownies. Cut into squares. Makes about 2 dozen.

Chocolate-Ganache-Topped Brownies

I have taught this brownie recipe for years and years and it never fails to elicit "oohs" and "ahs" from everyone—usually followed by "good chocolate does make a difference!" Lesson learned in advance—use only the very best chocolate for these decadent brownies. They will satisfy you, me, and anyone else who claims to be a demanding chocolate lover.

BROWNIE BASE

1 lb. semisweet chocolate, coarsely chopped
1 lb. bittersweet chocolate, coarsely chopped
1 cup unsalted butter, softened to room temperature
9 large eggs, lightly beaten
3 cups granulated sugar
1 tsp. pure vanilla extract
3 cups unbleached, all-purpose flour
½ tsp. salt

GANACHE

1 cup heavy (whipping) cream
12 oz. semisweet chocolate, finely chopped

BEV'S BITE

You want me to test these where? That's right, test 1 to 2" from the edge of the pan. Why? By the time the center is completely set, the edges will be dry. Look for very moist crumbs if you *must* test in the center!

Heat oven to 300 degrees. Lightly grease an 11x17" baking pan. Cover the bottom of the pan with a piece of parchment paper cut to fit. Lightly grease the parchment paper.

For the Brownie Base: Combine the chocolates in a double boiler set over simmering water. Stir often, over low heat, until mixture is melted and smooth.

Remove top of double boiler from heat, and carefully wipe bottom (so none of the moisture steams up into the chocolate mixture); cool slightly. Whisk in the butter to blend.

In a medium bowl with an electric mixer, beat the eggs, sugar, and vanilla on low speed until combined.

Add the cooled chocolate mixture to the egg mixture. Gently add in flour and salt just until mixture is combined. Spread into prepared pan. Bake for 15 to 20 minutes or until a cake tester or toothpick comes out with a few moist crumbs attached, testing 1 to 2" from the edge of the pan. Cool pan completely on a wire rack.

For the Ganache: Bring the cream to a boil in a medium saucepan. Remove from the heat and whisk in the chocolate. When the brownies have thoroughly cooled, invert the pan over a wire rack placed atop waxed paper. Remove the parchment paper. Spread the ganache evenly over the brownies. Place brownies in the refrigerator to set. Cut into bars once cooled and ganache has firmed slightly. Makes about 1½ dozen.

Chunky Brownies

Chocolate upon chocolate, moist, nut textured, and intensely flavored—these brownies are sure to satisfy!

BROWNIE BASE
1½ cups unsalted butter
3 cups granulated sugar
1 tbsp. pure vanilla extract
6 large eggs, lightly beaten
1½ cups unbleached, all-purpose flour
¾ cup unsweetened cocoa powder, sifted
¾ tsp. salt
12 oz. semisweet chocolate, coarsely chopped
1½ cups chopped pecans or walnuts, toasted

Heat oven to 350 degrees. Lightly grease an 11x15" *insulated* baking pan.

For the Brownie Base: Melt the butter in a medium saucepan over low heat. Remove the saucepan from the heat, then whisk in sugar, vanilla, and eggs, blending well.

Whisk in flour, cocoa, and salt, mixing well. Add chocolate pieces and nuts. Spread into prepared pan. Bake for 30 minutes or until a cake tester or toothpick inserted near the center comes out with a few moist crumbs attached. Brownies will be dry if over-baked! Cool pan completely on a wire rack. Cut into bars. Makes about 3 dozen.

Classic Mix of Chocolates Brownies

You may think this is a little crazy, but freezing these brownies for 30 minutes before cutting and serving brings out the fudgy texture!

BROWNIE BASE
½ cup unsalted butter
2 oz. unsweetened chocolate, coarsely chopped
2 oz. bittersweet chocolate, coarsely chopped
1¼ cups granulated sugar
1 tsp. pure vanilla extract
¼ tsp. salt
2 large eggs, lightly beaten
½ cup unbleached, all-purpose flour
½ cup semisweet chocolate chips

Heat oven to 375 degrees. Line an 8" square pan with foil; lightly grease the foil.

For the Brownie Base: Combine the butter with the chocolates in a medium saucepan over low heat, stirring constantly until the mixture is melted. Remove saucepan from heat.

Whisk in sugar, vanilla, and salt. Whisk in eggs, blending well. Gently add in flour just until combined.

Mix in chips. Spread into prepared pan. Bake for 30 to 35 minutes or until a cake tester or toothpick inserted near the center comes out with a few *wet* crumbs attached. Cool pan on a wire rack for 30 minutes, then place pan in freezer for 30 additional minutes.

Remove pan from freezer, remove foil from brownies, and cut brownies into squares. Makes about 1½ dozen.

Colossal Brownies

Sometimes it's just plain fun to make eye-popping, immense, larger-than-life brownies!

BROWNIE BASE

6 oz. unsweetened chocolate, coarsely chopped
2 oz. bittersweet chocolate, coarsely chopped
1 cup unsalted butter, softened to room temperature
3 cups granulated sugar
6 large eggs, lightly beaten
1¾ cups unbleached, all-purpose flour
1½ tsp. pure vanilla extract
½ tsp. salt
2 cups large pecan pieces, toasted

BEV'S BITES

So how would you get large pecan pieces? Easily—just break pecan halves apart with your fingers.

My cutting suggestion: cut pan of brownies lengthwise into thirds, then crosswise into fifths.

Brownies freeze well. Store these, well wrapped, in the freezer for up to 1 month.

Heat oven to 350 degrees. Lightly grease a 15½ x 10½" jellyroll pan.

For the Brownie Base: Combine the chocolates in a double boiler set over simmering water. Stir often, over low heat, until mixture is melted and smooth.

Remove top of double boiler from heat, and carefully wipe bottom (so none of the moisture steams up into the chocolate mixture). Whisk in butter, sugar, and eggs until blended.

Blend in flour, vanilla, and salt. Stir in pecan pieces. Spread into prepared pan. Bake for 20 to 25 minutes or until a cake tester or toothpick inserted in the center comes out with a few moist crumbs attached. Cool pan completely on a wire rack. Cut into colossal-size pieces. Makes about 1 dozen.

Crusty-Top, Soft-Center Brownies

A sweet crust and a chewy center provide a delicious combo of flavors and textures! I even had a "brownie moment" not too long ago and decided to bake these on the grill. They turned out beautifully!

BROWNIE BASE

3 oz. unsweetened chocolate, coarsely chopped
½ cup unsalted butter, softened to room temperature
1¼ cups granulated sugar
¼ cup firmly packed light brown sugar
1½ tsp. pure vanilla extract
3 large eggs, lightly beaten
1½ cups unbleached, all-purpose flour
¼ teaspoon salt

BEV'S BITE ——————

If you want tender brownies with a cake-like consistency, stir the brownie batter only until smooth; do not overmix.

Heat oven to 350 degrees. Grease *bottom only* of an 8" square pan.

For the Brownie Base: Melt the chocolate in a double boiler set over simmering water. Stir often, over low heat, until chocolate is melted and smooth.

Remove top of double boiler from heat, and carefully wipe bottom (so none of the moisture steams up into the chocolate mixture). Whisk in butter, sugars, and vanilla to blend. Whisk in eggs; mix well. Gently add in flour and salt just until mixture is combined. Spread into prepared pan. Bake for 25 to 30 minutes or until a cake tester or toothpick inserted near the center comes out with a few moist crumbs attached. Brownies will be dry if overbaked! Cool pan completely on a wire rack. Cut into bars. Makes about 2 dozen.

Deluxe Brownies with Caramel Sauce

Take a classic brownie, add a classic sauce and ice cream, and—voila!—you have an extraordinary classic brownie treat!

DELUXE BROWNIE BASE
7 oz. unsweetened chocolate, coarsely chopped
¾ cup + 2 tbsp. unsalted butter
4 large eggs, lightly beaten
1½ cups granulated sugar
½ cup superfine sugar
1¼ tsp. pure vanilla extract
1½ cups cake flour, sifted
¾ tsp. baking powder
½ tsp. salt

CARAMEL SAUCE
1 cup firmly packed dark brown sugar
1 cup heavy (whipping) cream
¼ cup rice syrup or light corn syrup
2 tbsp. unsalted butter
1 tbsp. pure vanilla extract

Ice cream, flavor of your choice

BEV'S BITES
My Brownie Base is Disappearing Brownies (see index) with pecans omitted.

Leftover sauce? Store in a covered container in the refrigerator for up to 2 weeks.

Heat oven to 325 degrees. Lightly grease a 13x9" baking pan.

For the Brownie Base: Melt the chocolate and butter in a medium saucepan over low heat, stirring until smooth. Cool slightly.

In a large bowl with an electric mixer, beat eggs and sugars on high speed until mixture is light, fluffy, and lemon colored, stopping occasionally and scraping sides of bowl. Add chocolate/butter mixture and vanilla, beating on low speed until combined.

Add flour, baking powder, and salt, beating on low speed until combined, stopping and scraping sides of bowl as needed. Spread into prepared pan. Bake for 25 to 30 minutes or until a cake tester or toothpick comes out with a few moist crumbs attached, testing 1 to 2" from the edge of the pan. Cool pan completely on a wire rack. Cut into 3 to 3½" pieces.

For the Caramel Sauce: Combine sugar, cream, syrup, and butter in a medium saucepan. Bring to a boil, stirring occasionally. Reduce heat; boil gently until slightly thickened (this will take 5 to 10 minutes). Remove from heat; stir in vanilla. Serve warm. Makes 2½ cups.

To serve this deluxe dessert, place brownie piece in a wide serving bowl. Top with a scoop of ice cream, then sauce. Entire recipe will serve 10+.

Disappearing Brownies

You'll know they're good because they'll disappear like magic!

BROWNIE BASE

7 oz. unsweetened chocolate, coarsely
   chopped
¾ cup + 2 tbsp. unsalted butter
4 large eggs, lightly beaten
1½ cups granulated sugar
½ cup superfine sugar
1¼ tsp. pure vanilla extract
1½ cups cake flour, sifted
¾ tsp. baking powder
½ tsp. salt
1¼ cups coarsely chopped pecans,
   toasted

BEV'S BITE ———————

Why cake flour? It's a fine-textured, soft
wheat flour that makes for particularly
tender brownies and cakes.

Heat oven to 325 degrees. Lightly grease a 13x9" baking pan.

For the Brownie Base: Melt the chocolate and butter in a small saucepan over low heat, stirring until smooth. Cool slightly.

In a large bowl with an electric mixer, beat eggs and sugars on high speed until mixture is light, fluffy, and lemon colored, stopping occasionally and scraping sides of bowl. Add chocolate/butter mixture and vanilla, beating on low speed until combined.

Add flour, baking powder, and salt, beating on low speed until combined, stopping and scraping sides of bowl as needed. Gently stir in pecans. Spread into prepared pan. Bake for 25 to 30 minutes or until a cake tester or toothpick comes out with a few moist crumbs attached, testing 1 to 2" from the edge of the pan. Cool pan completely on a wire rack. Cut into bars. Makes about 1½ dozen.

Filled and Frosted Rocky Road

I know, I know . . . this has lots of steps, but it is well worth your time and effort. An East Coast chef/baker friend of mine shared this recipe with me (she created it for her deli), and she guarantees that once your guests try these, you'll be declared the Filled and Frosted Rocky Road King or Queen of anywhere!

BROWNIE BASE
2 oz. unsweetened chocolate, coarsely chopped
½ cup unsalted butter, softened to room temperature
1¼ cups unbleached, all-purpose flour
1 cup granulated sugar
1 tsp. baking powder
1 tsp. pure vanilla extract
2 large eggs, lightly beaten
¾ cup chopped roasted peanuts

ROCKY ROAD FILLING
10 oz. cream cheese, softened to room temperature
½ cup granulated sugar
2 tbsp. unbleached, all-purpose flour
½ tsp. pure vanilla or chocolate extract
1 large egg, lightly beaten
¼ cup chopped roasted peanuts
1 cup semisweet chocolate chips
2 cups mini marshmallows

ROCKY ROAD FROSTING
½ cup unsalted butter
1 oz. unsweetened chocolate, coarsely chopped
3 cups confectioners' sugar, sifted
¼ cup milk, whole or 2 percent, room temperature
1 tsp. pure vanilla extract

Heat oven to 350 degrees. Lightly grease and flour a 13x9" baking pan, tapping out any excess flour.

For the Brownie Base: Melt the chocolate in a double boiler set over simmering water. Stir often, over low heat, until chocolate is melted and smooth.

Remove top of double boiler from heat, and carefully wipe bottom (so none of the moisture steams up into the chocolate). Whisk in butter, flour, sugar, baking powder, vanilla, and eggs; mix well. Gently stir in nuts. Spread into prepared pan.

For the Rocky Road Filling: In a medium bowl with an electric mixer, beat cream cheese, sugar, flour, vanilla, and egg at medium speed until smooth and fluffy. Gently stir in nuts. Spread over chocolate batter; sprinkle with chocolate chips. Bake for 25 to 35 minutes or until a cake tester or toothpick inserted in the center comes out with a few moist crumbs attached.

Immediately sprinkle marshmallows over top. Return to oven and bake an additional 3 minutes.

For the Rocky Road Frosting: Combine the butter and chocolate in a medium saucepan over medium-low heat, stirring until mixture is melted and smooth. Remove from heat.

Beat in sugar, milk, and vanilla with an electric mixer on medium-low speed until smooth. Immediately pour frosting over marshmallows. Chill at least 1 hour until firm. Cut into bars. Makes about 3 dozen.

I Love Rocky Road! Brownies

How did this name come about? Every time my friends and I gather round to eat these, we join in for a chorus of that Weird Al song, "I Love Rocky Road"... instant, tasty entertainment. These are rich brownies topped with all your favorites. How can you not love them?

BROWNIE BASE
½ cup unsalted butter
2 oz. unsweetened chocolate, coarsely chopped
2 large eggs
1 cup granulated sugar
⅔ cup unbleached, all-purpose flour
¼ tsp. salt
1 tsp. pure vanilla extract

ROCKY ROAD TOPPING
½ cup chopped salted peanuts
½ cup semisweet or milk chocolate chips
1 cup mini marshmallows
¼ cup Smooth and Silky Fudge Sauce (see index)

Heat oven to 350 degrees. Lightly grease a 9" square pan.

For the Brownie Base: Melt butter and chocolate in a small saucepan over low heat, stirring until smooth. Set aside to cool.

In a medium bowl with an electric mixer, beat eggs at medium speed until thick and lemon colored. Continue beating and add the chocolate/butter mixture, sugar, flour, salt, and vanilla, stopping and scraping bowl often, until ingredients are well mixed. Spread into prepared pan. Bake for 20 to 25 minutes or until a cake tester or toothpick inserted near the center comes out with a few moist crumbs attached.

For the Rocky Road Topping: Sprinkle nuts, chips, and marshmallows over hot brownies. Drizzle with sauce. Continue baking for 12 to 15 minutes or until lightly browned. Cool pan completely on a wire rack. Cut into squares. Makes 18+.

Swirled Brownies

Dense, fudgy brownies—this time with a swirl of sour cream to create that oh-so-special marbled effect. These are perfect to add variety when you're serving an assortment of brownies.

BROWNIE BASE

4 oz. unsweetened chocolate, coarsely chopped
½ cup unsalted butter, softened to room temperature
1½ cups granulated sugar
½ cup firmly packed light brown sugar
½ cup sour cream
4 large eggs, lightly beaten
2 tsp. pure vanilla extract
1½ cups unbleached, all-purpose flour
1 tsp. baking powder
½ tsp. salt

SWIRLIN'

½ cup sour cream, room temperature
½ cup granulated sugar
1 large egg, lightly beaten
2 tbsp. unbleached, all-purpose flour

BEV'S BITE

Yes, you *could* use light or low-fat sour cream in this recipe, but here's my suggestion. Use regular sour cream, enjoy the satisfying flavors, eat fewer, then take a long walk. (No, you *can't* take extra brownies with you on that walk!)

Heat oven to 350 degrees. Lightly grease a 13x9" baking pan.

For the Brownie Base: Melt the chocolate in a double boiler set over simmering water. Stir often, over low heat, until chocolate is melted and smooth.

Remove top of double boiler from heat, and carefully wipe bottom (so none of the moisture steams up into the chocolate).

With a whisk or large spoon, stir in butter, sugars, sour cream, eggs, and vanilla; mix well. Gently add in flour, baking powder, and salt just until mixture is combined. Spread ⅔ *of the batter* into prepared pan.

For the Swirlin': Whisk ingredients together in a small bowl until smooth. Spread atop Brownie Base in pan, then spoon remaining Brownie Base over top.

To swirl batters, drag a knife in a zigzag motion across entire surface. Bake for 40 to 50 minutes or until a cake tester or toothpick inserted in the center comes out with a few moist crumbs attached. Cool pan completely on a wire rack. Cut into bars. Makes about 3 dozen.

Many Swirls Brownies

Is this a brownie? Yes! Is this a cheesecake? Well, yes! It's the perfect combination of flavors and textures for the brownie cheesecake lover in all of us.

CREAM BASE
12 oz. cream cheese, softened to room temperature
¼ cup confectioners' sugar, sifted
¼ cup granulated sugar
1 tsp. pure vanilla extract
1 large egg, lightly beaten
⅛ tsp. salt

BROWNIE BASE
1 cup unsalted butter
2 oz. unsweetened chocolate, coarsely chopped
6 oz. semisweet or bittersweet chocolate, coarsely chopped
1 tsp. unsweetened cocoa powder, sifted
2 tsp. pure vanilla extract
1½ cups granulated sugar
3 tbsp. rice syrup or light corn syrup
4 large eggs, lightly beaten
1 large egg yolk, lightly beaten
1 cup unbleached, all-purpose flour
1 tsp. baking powder
½ tsp. salt
4½ oz. white chocolate, coarsely chopped

BEV'S BITES
*Okay, so you've spent some serious time and effort making these brownies and now you have to wait overnight? Here's my solution—cut a small square for yourself to try (quality control!), then go for a long walk so you'll forget about the brownies until tomorrow!

Leftovers? Store tightly wrapped in the refrigerator.

Heat oven to 350 degrees. Line a 13x9" baking pan with foil. Lightly grease the foil.

For the Cream Base: In a medium bowl with an electric mixer, beat together all the ingredients until smooth.

For the Brownie Base: Melt the butter with the unsweetened and semisweet or bittersweet chocolates in a medium saucepan over low heat, until mixture is melted and smooth. Remove pan from heat; whisk in cocoa powder and vanilla.

Whisk sugar and syrup into butter/chocolate mixture until smooth. Add eggs and egg yolk, whisking until smooth and glossy. Stir in flour, baking powder, and salt, combining until smooth. Gently stir in the white chocolate pieces.

Spread *half the Brownie Base* into prepared pan. Drop table-spoonfuls of *half of the Cream Base* atop the Brownie Base. Lightly spread the remaining Brownie Base over the top. Drop tablespoonfuls of the remaining Cream Base on top and *gently* swirl both mixtures together (using a butter knife).

Bake brownies for 30 to 40 minutes or until a cake tester or toothpick inserted in the center comes out with a few moist crumbs attached. Brownies will be dry if overbaked! Cool pan completely on a wire rack.

You're not gonna be happy with me, but cover the pan once cool and place in the refrigerator overnight before cutting. This allows flavors to develop.*

When ready to cut, lift brownies out of the pan using the foil as a handle. Invert, gently peel off the foil, and then reinvert. Cut into squares. Makes about 2 dozen.

Count the many swirls while you're enjoying this brownie's moist, creamy flavors.

Old-Fashioned Brownies

A friend of mine named these after I created and served them to her, her thought being that cocoa power is old-fashioned. Whatever . . . there's nothing old-fashioned about how quick and easy these brownies are to make!

BROWNIE BASE
½ cup unsweetened cocoa powder, sifted
2 cups unbleached, all-purpose flour
2 cups granulated sugar
1 cup unsalted butter, softened to room temperature
2 large eggs, lightly beaten
1 tsp. pure vanilla extract
1 cup chopped walnuts or pecans, toasted, or mini semisweet chocolate chips

Heat oven to 350 degrees. Lightly grease a 13x9" baking pan.

In a large bowl with an electric mixer, beat cocoa, flour, sugar, butter, eggs, and vanilla at medium speed, stopping and scraping bowl often until well mixed.

Gently stir in nuts or chips. Spread into prepared pan. Bake for 20 to 25 minutes or until a cake tester or toothpick comes out with a few moist crumbs attached, testing 2" from the edge of the pan. Cool pan completely on a wire rack. Cut into bars. Makes about 3 dozen.

Piece-of-Cake Brownies

The Brownie Base for this recipe is one of the basics that I use as a springboard for other brownie recipes. Almonds are optional in the batter.

BROWNIE BASE
¼ cup unsalted butter
⅔ cup granulated sugar
¼ cup unsweetened cocoa powder, sifted
1 large egg, lightly beaten
½ tsp. pure vanilla extract
¾ cup unbleached, all-purpose flour
⅓ cup milk, whole or 2 percent
½ tsp. baking powder
¼ tsp. baking soda
¼ tsp. salt
⅓ cup chopped almonds
1 tsp. confectioners' sugar, sifted

CONFECTIONERS' SUGAR ICING
½ cup confectioners' sugar, sifted
1 tsp. unsweetened cocoa powder, sifted
¼ tsp. pure vanilla extract
1 tbsp. or more milk, whole or 2 percent

Heat oven to 350 degrees. Lightly grease a 9" square pan.

For the Brownie Base: Melt the butter in a medium saucepan. Remove from heat, whisking in sugar and cocoa powder until combined.

Blend the egg and vanilla into mixture in saucepan. Mix *just until* combined. Whisk in flour, milk, baking powder, baking soda, and salt, beating until well combined. Gently stir in almonds. Spread into prepared pan. Bake for 16 to 18 minutes or until a cake tester or toothpick inserted near the center comes out with a few moist crumbs attached. Cool pan completely on a wire rack. Sprinkle with confectioners' sugar.

For the Confectioners' Sugar Icing: Whisk together the sugar, cocoa powder, vanilla, and enough milk to make a drizzling consistency.

Drizzle Confectioners' Sugar Icing over Brownie Base and let stand 30 minutes to set. Cut into bars. Makes 18+.

Raspberry Marbled Brownies

Raspberries, cheesecake, and brownies . . . what a delicious combination of flavors! Try this with peach preserves, too, for a change of pace (and don't forget to rename!).

BROWNIE BASE

3 oz. semisweet chocolate, coarsely chopped

1 oz. bittersweet chocolate, coarsely chopped

¼ cup unsalted butter

2 large eggs, lightly beaten

¾ cup granulated sugar

½ tsp. pure vanilla extract

¾ cup unbleached, all-purpose flour

½ tsp. baking powder

¼ tsp. salt

CHEESECAKE BASE

8 oz. cream cheese, softened to room temperature

3 tbsp. confectioners' sugar, sifted

1 large egg, lightly beaten

½ tsp. pure vanilla extract

2 tbsp. seedless raspberry preserves

Heat oven to 325 degrees. Lightly grease a 9" square pan.

For the Brownie Base: Melt the chocolates and butter in a medium saucepan over low heat until melted, stirring until smooth. Remove from heat.

Whisk in eggs, sugar, and vanilla. Gently add flour, baking powder, and salt just until mixture is combined. Reserving *1 cup* of the Brownie Base, spread remaining Brownie Base into prepared pan.

For the Cheesecake Base: In a medium bowl with an electric mixer, beat cream cheese until smooth, stopping occasionally to scrape sides of bowl. Beat in sugar, egg, and vanilla on medium speed until well combined. Spread over Brownie Base, then drop tablespoonfuls of remaining Brownie Base on Cheesecake Base. Drop raspberry preserves (using a small spoon) in the spaces where there is no Brownie Base. (Stop and think about it . . . this isn't as confusing as it sounds.)

Swirl gently with a thin spatula to create a marbled pattern. Bake for 40 minutes or until a cake tester or toothpick inserted near the center comes out with a few moist crumbs attached. Cool pan completely on a wire rack. Cut into bars. Makes about 1 dozen.

Saucepan Brownies

These use a similar technique (on a smaller scale) as do my Plain and Simple Fudgy Brownies—brownie batter is stirred up in a saucepan, then poured and baked! Sensationally easy.

BROWNIE BASE
½ cup unsalted butter
2 oz. unsweetened chocolate, coarsely
   chopped
1 cup granulated sugar
1 tsp. pure vanilla extract
2 large eggs, lightly beaten
⅔ cup unbleached, all-purpose flour
½ tsp. baking powder
¼ tsp. salt
½ cup chopped nuts, if desired (hazelnuts, pecans, walnuts, or almonds)

Heat oven to 350 degrees. Grease and lightly flour an 8" square pan.

Melt the butter and chocolate in a medium saucepan over low heat, stirring constantly. Remove from heat; cool slightly. Whisk in sugar and vanilla. Blend in eggs.

Whisk in flour, baking powder, and salt until blended. Gently stir in nuts. Spread into prepared pan. Bake for 20 to 25 minutes or until a cake tester or toothpick inserted in the center comes out with a few moist crumbs attached. Cool pan completely on a wire rack. Cut into bars. Makes about 1½ dozen.

BEV'S BITE ———

Like your brownies frosted? There are lots of options to top this recipe in the "Frostings and Glazes" chapter.

Stress-Free Brownies

What makes these stress free? They can be eaten right out of the freezer, so you don't have to go through the stress of thinking about thawing them first!

BROWNIE BASE

1 cup unsalted butter

6 oz. semisweet chocolate, coarsely chopped

4 oz. unsweetened chocolate, coarsely chopped

3 large eggs, lightly beaten

1 cup + 2 tbsp. granulated sugar

1 tbsp. pure vanilla extract

½ cup unbleached, all-purpose flour

1½ tsp. baking powder

½ tsp. salt

1½ cups semisweet chocolate chips or coarsely chopped bittersweet chocolate

1½ cups coarsely chopped walnuts, toasted

Heat oven to 350 degrees. Lightly grease an 11x8" baking pan, dusting lightly with flour. (Be sure to tap out any excess flour.)

Melt the butter in a medium saucepan over low heat. Add semisweet and unsweetened chocolates, stirring over very low heat until the chocolates are melted. Remove saucepan from heat.

In a medium bowl with an electric mixer, beat eggs and sugar on medium-high speed until very thick and smooth. Gently mix in vanilla and melted chocolate.

Blend flour, baking powder, and salt into egg/chocolate batter with a spatula. Gently add chocolate chips or chocolate pieces and nuts. Spread into prepared pan. Bake for 35 to 40 minutes or until a cake tester or toothpick inserted near the center comes out with a few moist crumbs attached. Do not overbake; you want the brownies a little gooey so they're a nice, fudgy consistency!

Cool pan completely on a wire rack. Cut into squares. Freeze after tasting a few (you're responsible for quality control, remember!). Makes about 2 dozen.

Lighten up. You can never have too much chocolate (of any kind) in, atop, or curled beside your brownies.

White Chocolate Glazed Fudge Brownies

These brownies are rich and fudgy, and the white chocolate glaze makes a zebralike contrast! Always a favorite at my house, they're easy to make and yield spectacular results.

BROWNIE BASE

2 oz. unsweetened chocolate, coarsely chopped

2 oz. bittersweet chocolate, coarsely chopped

½ cup unsalted butter, softened to room temperature

2 cups granulated sugar

4 large eggs, lightly beaten

2 tsp. pure vanilla extract

1 cup unbleached, all-purpose flour

¼ tsp. salt

WHITE CHOCOLATE GLAZE

2 oz. white chocolate, coarsely chopped

1 tbsp. unsalted butter, softened to room temperature

1 tbsp. or more heavy (whipping) cream

Heat oven to 350 degrees. Lightly grease a 13x9" baking pan.

For the Brownie Base: Combine the chocolates in a double boiler set over simmering water. Stir often, over low heat, until mixture is melted and smooth.

Remove top of double boiler from heat, carefully wipe bottom (so none of the moisture steams up into the chocolate mixture), and set mixture aside to cool slightly.

In a medium bowl with an electric mixer, combine butter, sugar, eggs, and vanilla, beating on medium speed until light and fluffy. On low speed, blend in flour, salt, and chocolate mixture. Spread into prepared pan. Bake for 30 to 35 minutes or until a cake tester or toothpick inserted in the center comes out with a few moist crumbs attached. Brownies will be dry if overbaked! Cool pan completely on a wire rack.

For the White Chocolate Glaze: Melt the chocolate with butter in a small saucepan over low heat, stirring constantly until smooth, adding cream as needed for a smooth "drizzle" consistency. Drizzle glaze over brownies. Let stand until set, then cut into bars. Makes about 3 dozen.

Tri-Chocolate Brownies

My culinary students always tell me that the only thing better than a brownie of mine with one or two chocolates in it is (you guessed it) a brownie of mine with three chocolates. These brownies are dark and dense and—oh!—so chocolaty.

BROWNIE BASE
Unsweetened cocoa powder, sifted
2 oz. semisweet or bittersweet chocolate, coarsely chopped
2 oz. unsweetened chocolate, coarsely chopped
6 tbsp. unsalted butter, softened to room temperature
¾ cup granulated sugar
1 tsp. pure vanilla extract
2 large eggs, lightly beaten
½ cup unbleached, all-purpose flour
½ tsp. salt
½ cup semisweet chocolate chips

BEV'S BITE ───────────

By combining several different types of chocolates in a brownie recipe, you mix flavor profiles and textures.

Heat oven to 350 degrees. Lightly grease an 8" square pan. Sprinkle bottom with cocoa powder, tapping out any excess.

Combine the semisweet or bittersweet and unsweetened chocolates in a double boiler set over simmering water. Stir often, over low heat, until mixture is melted and smooth.

Remove top of double boiler from heat, carefully wipe bottom (so none of the moisture steams up into the chocolate mixture), and set mixture aside to cool for 15 minutes.

Whisk in butter, sugar, and vanilla until blended. Whisk in eggs, beating until smooth. Gently add in flour and salt just until mixture is combined. Stir in chocolate chips. Spread into prepared pan. Bake for 20 to 30 minutes or until a cake tester or toothpick inserted near the center comes out with a few moist crumbs attached. Cool pan completely on a wire rack. Cut into squares. Makes about 1½ dozen.

Your Momma's Buttermilk Brownies

If your momma made these, you'd be a very popular kid! These are moist, flavorful brownies with a smooth frosting.

BROWNIE BASE
½ cup unsalted butter, softened to room temperature
1 cup water
2 cups unbleached, all-purpose flour
2 cups granulated sugar
2 tbsp. unsweetened cocoa powder, sifted
½ cup buttermilk
1 tsp. baking soda
2 large eggs, lightly beaten

MOMMA'S FROSTING
¼ cup unsweetened cocoa powder, sifted
⅓ cup buttermilk, room temperature
½ cup unsalted butter, softened to room temperature
4½ cups confectioners' sugar, sifted
1 tsp. pure vanilla extract

Heat oven to 375 degrees. Lightly grease a 15x10x1" baking pan.

For the Brownie Base: Place the butter in a large mixing bowl. Bring water to a boil in a medium saucepan. Pour water over butter, stirring until butter is melted.

With an electric mixer at low speed, add flour, sugar, and cocoa powder and beat until blended. Beat at medium-high speed until smooth. Add buttermilk, baking soda, and eggs, blending well on low speed. Spread into prepared pan. Bake for 15 to 20 minutes or until a cake tester or toothpick inserted in the center comes out with a few moist crumbs attached. Cool pan completely on a wire rack.

For Momma's Frosting: Combine cocoa and buttermilk in a large saucepan. Bring to a boil over medium heat, whisking until smooth and blended. Remove from heat and add butter, stirring until butter is melted and combined. Whisk in sugar and vanilla until mixture is smooth and spreadable. Frost cooled brownies. Cut into bars. Makes about 4 dozen.

BEV'S BITE
No buttermilk in the house? Don't panic. To substitute, combine 1 tbsp. lemon juice or apple-cider vinegar with 1 cup whole or 2 percent milk. Let stand at room temperature for 15 minutes, then stir, measure, and use.

TOP 'EM OFF

*Why bury the cashews in the batter when you can show 'em off in
Caramel Brownies Studded with Cashews?*

All the Time in the World Caramel Sauce

This caramel sauce is phenomenal—and delicious atop brownies (or drizzled atop fresh apple slices while they're baking). Remember when your mom made you caramel apples? Me neither. This recipe makes up for the neglect! Special Note: You will need a clip-on candy thermometer and a pastry brush to make this recipe.

CARAMEL SAUCE

1 lb. dark brown sugar
1 cup unsalted butter, softened to
    room temperature
14-oz. can sweetened condensed milk
²⁄₃ cup dark corn syrup
¹⁄₃ cup pure maple syrup (don't even
    think about substituting imitation
    syrup!)
½ tsp. pure vanilla extract
1 tsp. light molasses (Barbados)
¼ tsp. salt

BEV'S BITES

For the caramel to be silky smooth, the sugar must be completely dissolved.

Around our house we have a little cautionary "joke." Whenever something comes off the burner or out of the oven, or has just been cooked and is likely to burn you, we'll say to one another, "That's really hot—don't put your tongue on it!" As you cook this caramel, the aroma will drive you crazy and you simply will be counting the moments until it's done and you can lick the spoon, dip your fingers into the saucepan, or swipe a few drops off the thermometer while it's cooling. My advice to you is, until the mixture and all the surrounding remains reach temperatures *below 200 degrees,* "don't put your tongue or any other part of your body on it—it's *really* hot!"

For the Caramel Sauce: Combine all the ingredients in a 3-qt. saucepan. (Saucepan needs to be at least 3" deep to allow for expansion of the mixture while cooking.) Stir mixture with a wooden spoon over medium-low heat until sugar dissolves. (The easiest way to test this is to *carefully* rub a little caramel between two fingers—if no sugar crystals are felt the sugar is dissolved.) Occasionally brush down sides of pan with a wet pastry brush. This process takes about 15 minutes or more.

Attach a clip-on thermometer to the side of the saucepan. Increase heat to medium high; cook caramel at a rolling boil until thermometer registers 236 degrees. Stir constantly but with a heatproof spatula this time, and continue to brush down sides of pan with a wet pastry brush. Pour caramel into a heatproof bowl (glass, metal, or ceramic). Do not scrape saucepan. Place thermometer into caramel; cool to 200 degrees. Do not stir.

At this point, sauce may be used or cooled completely then covered tightly and stored in the refrigerator for future use. Makes about 4½ cups.

In a Hurry Caramel Sauce

Just a few ingredients and a quick stir or two make a luscious, versatile caramel sauce. This thickens slightly upon cooling but will not harden.

CARAMEL SAUCE
½ cup unsalted butter
1¼ cups firmly packed light brown sugar
2 tbsp. brown rice syrup
½ cup heavy (whipping) cream

For the Caramel Sauce: Melt the butter in a medium saucepan. Whisk in sugar and syrup. Bring mixture to a boil, cooking and stirring until sugar dissolves.

Stir in cream; return mixture to a boil. Remove sauce from heat and let cool slightly before using. Makes about 2½ cups.

BEV'S BITES
So what is brown rice syrup? It is a natural sweetener (and a great substitute for corn syrup). It is a mildly sweet, caramel-flavored, golden syrup made from rice. You should find it at specialty grocery and natural-food stores.

Leftovers? Store, covered, in the refrigerator.

Nuts 'n' Caramel Brownies

Wow! Pecans, chocolate, and caramel. Ladies and gentlemen, start your ovens. . . .

BROWNIE BASE
4 oz. semisweet chocolate, coarsely chopped
¼ cup firmly packed light brown sugar
¾ cup granulated sugar
1 cup unsalted butter, softened to room temperature
3 large eggs, lightly beaten
1 tsp. pure vanilla extract
1½ cups unbleached, all-purpose flour
¾ cup coarsely chopped pecans, toasted
8 to 9 oz. milk chocolate, coarsely chopped
¾ cup coarsely chopped walnuts, toasted

CARAMEL LAYER
1½ cups In a Hurry Caramel Sauce (see index)

Heat oven to 350 degrees. Lightly grease a 13x9" baking pan.

For the Brownie Base: Melt the semisweet chocolate in a double boiler set over simmering water. Stir often, over low heat, until chocolate is melted and smooth.

Remove top of double boiler from heat, and carefully wipe bottom (so none of the moisture steams up into the chocolate); cool.

In a large bowl with an electric mixer, combine sugars and butter, beating until light and fluffy. Beat in melted chocolate, eggs, and vanilla; mix well.

Add flour and mix just until combined, scraping bowl as needed. Gently stir in pecans. Spread *half* the batter into prepared pan. Bake for 18 minutes.

For the Caramel Layer: While Brownie Base is baking, warm caramel to a pourable consistency.

Remove Brownie Base from oven and sprinkle milk chocolate over hot, partially baked base. Carefully drizzle caramel mixture over chocolate. Spread remaining Brownie Base over caramel (gently now, covering whatever is possible). Sprinkle walnuts over top.

Bake for 25 minutes or until a cake tester or toothpick comes out with a few moist crumbs attached, testing 1" from the edge of the pan. Cool pan completely on a wire rack. Refrigerate a minimum of 2 hours. (*Sorry!* Caramel needs to set up!) Cut into bars. Makes about 2½ dozen.

To-Die-For Brownies with Pecan-Studded Caramel Sauce

Is this my signature brownie? Aren't they all? This particular recipe makes a fudgy, moist, and rich brownie that I've topped with a soft, smooth caramel sauce. Then, just 'cause I'm nuts about nuts, I've added toasted pecans.

BROWNIE BASE
10 oz. bittersweet chocolate, coarsely chopped
¾ cup unsalted butter, softened to room temperature
2 cups firmly packed light brown sugar
1 cup granulated sugar
2½ tsp. pure vanilla extract
1 tsp. unsweetened cocoa powder, sifted
½ tsp. salt
5 large eggs, lightly beaten
1½ cups unbleached, all-purpose flour

PECAN-STUDDED CARAMEL SAUCE
2½ cups In a Hurry Caramel Sauce (see index)
2½ cups salted pecan halves, toasted

Heat oven to 350 degrees. Lightly grease a 13x9" baking pan.

For the Brownie Base: Melt the chocolate in a double boiler set over simmering water. Stir often, over low heat, until chocolate is smooth.

Remove top of double boiler from heat, and carefully wipe bottom (so none of the moisture steams up into the chocolate); cool to room temperature.

In a large bowl with an electric mixer, beat butter, sugars, vanilla, cocoa powder, and salt until well combined, scraping bowl as needed. With mixer on low, gradually add cooled melted chocolate and eggs, beating well after each addition. (Bowl may need a scrape or two occasionally.) Mix in flour, a little at a time, until combined. Spread into prepared pan. Bake for 30 to 35 minutes or until a toothpick or cake tester inserted near the center comes out with a few moist crumbs attached. Cool pan completely on a wire rack. Cut into bars. Makes 2 dozen.

For the Pecan-Studded Caramel Sauce: Rewarm caramel in a medium saucepan over low heat until pourable. Remove saucepan from heat. Stir in nuts.

Serve a brownie (or two!) with a generous helping of Pecan-Studded Caramel Sauce. Mmm!

Caramel Pecan-Topped Brownies

Sticky, gooey caramel pecan topping layered over this Brownie Base will remind you of chocolate "turtle" candies.

BROWNIE BASE
4 oz. semisweet chocolate, coarsely chopped
1 oz. unsweetened chocolate, coarsely chopped
½ cup unsalted butter, softened to room temperature
1 cup firmly packed light brown sugar
1 tsp. pure vanilla extract
3 large eggs, lightly beaten
1 cup unbleached, all-purpose flour
½ tsp. baking powder
¼ tsp. salt

CARAMEL PECAN TOPPING
1 cup All the Time in the World Caramel Sauce (see index)
1½ cups coarsely chopped pecans, toasted
2 oz. milk chocolate, coarsely chopped

Heat oven to 350 degrees. Lightly grease and flour a 9" square pan.

For the Brownie Base: Combine the chocolates in a double boiler set over simmering water. Stir often, over low heat, until mixture is melted and smooth.

Remove top of double boiler from heat, and carefully wipe bottom (so none of the moisture steams up into the chocolate mixture). Cool mixture to lukewarm. Whisk in butter, sugar, and vanilla until smooth. Whisk in eggs, beating well.

Add in flour, baking powder, and salt just until mixture is combined. Spread into prepared pan. Bake for 25 to 30 minutes or until a cake tester or toothpick comes out with a few moist crumbs attached, testing 1" from the edge of the pan. Cool pan completely on a wire rack.

For the Caramel Pecan Topping: In a small saucepan, heat caramel until pourable. Spread atop cooled Brownie Base and immediately scatter pecans atop caramel. Cool completely. When cool, melt chocolate and drizzle atop caramel. Chill in the refrigerator, loosely covered, until caramel and chocolate are firm (unfortunately, this takes at least 2 hours!).

Now your reward: Cut chilled brownies into squares and remove from the pan while still cold. In a perfect world, let brownies come to room temperature before eating! (Honestly, they do taste better at room temperature—but I recommend eating them chilled also so you can make an educated brownie decision.) Makes about 16 "turtles."

Caramel Brownies Studded with Cashews

Cashews, caramel, and chocolate are even more irresistible than pecans, caramel, and chocolate. But don't take my word for it— bake up a batch and taste.

BROWNIE BASE

2 oz. unsweetened chocolate, coarsely chopped

1 oz. bittersweet chocolate, coarsely chopped

1½ cups firmly packed light brown sugar

¾ cup unsalted butter, softened to room temperature

3 large eggs, lightly beaten

2½ tsp. pure vanilla extract

1¼ cups unbleached, all-purpose flour

¼ tsp. salt

8 oz. semisweet chocolate, coarsely chopped

1½ cups roasted, salted cashews, coarsely chopped

CARAMEL TOPPING

½ cup All the Time in the World Caramel Sauce (see index)

3 tbsp. heavy (whipping) cream or half-and-half

Heat oven to 325 degrees. Line two 8" square pans with foil; lightly grease foil.

For the Brownie Base: Combine the unsweetened and bittersweet chocolates in a double boiler set over simmering water. Stir often, over low heat, until mixture is melted and smooth.

Remove top of double boiler from heat, and carefully wipe bottom (so none of the moisture steams up into the chocolate mixture). Cool slightly.

Beat sugar and butter in a large bowl with an electric mixer until light and fluffy. Add eggs; beat well to combine. Stir in chocolates and vanilla, mixing well. Gently add in flour and salt just until mixture is combined. Stir in semisweet chocolate pieces. Divide batter evenly between prepared pans. "Stud" cashews atop Brownie Base. Bake for 20 to 25 minutes or until a cake tester or toothpick inserted near the center comes out with a few moist crumbs attached. Cool pans completely on a wire rack. Remove brownies from pans and gently peel off foil.

For the Caramel Topping: Combine the ingredients in a small saucepan. Stir frequently over low heat until smooth. Drizzle over brownies. Cool completely. Cut into squares. Makes about 3 dozen.

BEV'S BITES

You know those times when you're asked to bring dessert and you look longingly at the dish and wish you could just keep it at home and say you forgot? Well, not to worry. Since this makes two pans, bring one *and* leave one home. Now you're making two people happy!

By the way, my husband, John, says this is the "best bowl-lickin' batter!"

Atomic Brownies

Some things are just out of this world! This brownie recipe has been in my baking repertoire for many, many years, and it always wins raves. These brownies were named by one of my taste testers who, after a few bites (and asking for seconds), claimed their intense chocolate and espresso flavors were nothing short of atomic.

BROWNIE BASE
1 cup unsalted butter
14 oz. semisweet chocolate, coarsely chopped
4 oz. unsweetened chocolate, coarsely chopped
½ cup firmly packed dark brown sugar
½ cup firmly packed light brown sugar
⅔ cup granulated sugar
5 large eggs, lightly beaten
2 tsp. pure vanilla extract
1 tsp. milk, whole or 2 percent
1½ cups unbleached, all-purpose flour
2 tsp. instant espresso powder
¼ tsp. salt
1¼ cups coarsely chopped walnuts, toasted

CHOCOLATE DRIZZLER
⅓ cup heavy (whipping) cream
3 oz. bittersweet chocolate, finely chopped
2 oz. semisweet chocolate, finely chopped

Heat oven to 350 degrees. Line a 13x9" baking pan with foil, extending up and beyond the sides of the pan. Lightly (and gently so as not to tear it) grease foil.

For the Brownie Base: Combine the butter and chocolates in a large saucepan over low heat, stirring until mixture is melted and smooth. Whisk in sugars to blend.

Whisk in eggs, vanilla, and milk, blending until smooth. Add flour, espresso powder, and salt just until mixture is combined. Stir in nuts. Spread into prepared pan. Bake for 25 to 30 minutes or until a cake tester or toothpick inserted in the center comes out with a few moist crumbs attached. Cool pan completely on a wire rack. When cool, use foil ends to carefully lift brownies out of pan. Invert onto a clean cutting board, carefully remove foil, and then reinvert brownies. Return to a wire rack set atop a large piece of waxed paper.

For the Chocolate Drizzler: Bring cream to a simmer in a medium saucepan. Remove pan from heat and add chocolates. Let chocolates melt in hot cream for 2 minutes without stirring. Whisk until smooth. Cool Drizzler until thick but still soft and pourable. Pour over Brownie Base, allowing some to drip down and cover the sides (*now* you know the waxed paper is there for ease of cleanup and licking!). Spread Drizzler with a metal spatula, covering top and sides.

Let brownies firm up in the refrigerator. Cut into bars. Makes about 1½ dozen.

Let the celebration begin!

Brownies with Broiled Topping

Here is something a little different—a broiled peanut-butter topping on a cakelike brownie. Yum!

BROWNIE BASE
½ cup unsalted butter
3 oz. unsweetened chocolate, coarsely
   chopped
1 cup firmly packed light brown sugar
½ tsp. pure vanilla extract
2 large eggs, lightly beaten
½ cup unbleached, all-purpose flour
¼ cup mini semisweet chocolate chips

BROILED TOPPING
⅓ cup firmly packed light brown sugar
¾ cup crunchy peanut butter
2 tbsp. unsalted butter, melted
2 tbsp. half-and-half or milk

BEV'S BITE ——————————
My Brownie Base is Fudge Brownies (see
index).

Heat oven to 350 degrees. Lightly grease an 8" square pan.

For the Brownie Base: Combine the butter and chocolate in a large saucepan over low heat, stirring until mixture is melted and smooth. Remove saucepan from heat.

Beat in sugar and vanilla using a hand mixer. Add eggs; beat well.

Stir in flour, mixing until batter is smooth. Gently stir in chips. Spread into prepared pan. Bake for 25 minutes or until a cake tester or toothpick inserted near the center comes out with a few moist crumbs attached. Cool pan slightly on a wire rack.

For the Broiled Topping: Heat broiler. Combine all the ingredients in a small bowl, blending well.

Spread atop *warm* Brownie Base. Broil 4 to 6" from heat until bubbly and light golden brown. (This only takes a minute or two. Mixture burns easily, so don't be distracted—watch carefully!) Serve warm or cool. Cut into squares. Makes 9.

Chocolate Peanut Butter Brownies with Milk Chocolate Frosting

A chocolaty peanut-butter base and a creamy milk-chocolate frosting . . . are they done yet?

BROWNIE BASE

2 oz. unsweetened chocolate, coarsely chopped

½ cup unsalted butter, softened to room temperature

1¼ cups granulated sugar

3 large eggs, lightly beaten

1 tsp. pure vanilla extract

⅔ cup unbleached, all-purpose flour

½ tsp. baking powder

½ tsp. salt

½ cup crunchy peanut butter, softened to room temperature

4 oz. bittersweet chocolate, coarsely chopped

Milk Chocolate Frosting (see index)

Heat oven to 350 degrees. Lightly grease and flour a 9" square pan.

For the Brownie Base: Place unsweetened chocolate in a double boiler set over simmering water. Stir often, over low heat, until chocolate is melted.

Remove top of double boiler from heat, and carefully wipe bottom (so none of the moisture steams up into the chocolate). Cool to room temperature.

In a large bowl with an electric mixer on medium speed, beat butter and sugar until light and fluffy. Beat in eggs and vanilla, stopping to scrape down bowl as needed. Add flour, baking powder, and salt, stirring just until blended.

Add peanut butter and melted chocolate. Stir in bittersweet chocolate. Spread into prepared pan. Bake for 35 minutes or until a cake tester or toothpick inserted near the center comes out with a few moist crumbs attached. Cool pan completely on a wire rack.

For the Milk Chocolate Frosting: Frost cooled brownies. When frosting has set, cut into squares. Makes 12 to 16.

Peanut Butter Marbled Brownies

Peanut butter and chocolate are a great combo, and chunky peanut butter makes this extra special.

BROWNIE BASE

4 oz. unsweetened chocolate, coarsely chopped
^{2}/₃ cup unsalted butter
2 cups granulated sugar
4 large eggs, lightly beaten
1 tsp. pure vanilla extract
1¼ cups unbleached, all-purpose flour
1 tsp. baking powder
1 tsp. salt
4 to 5 oz. semisweet chocolate, coarsely chopped

PEANUT BUTTER MARBLE BASE

¾ cup crunchy peanut butter
⅓ cup unsalted butter, softened to room temperature
½ cup firmly packed light brown sugar
3 tbsp. unbleached, all-purpose flour
½ tsp. pure vanilla extract
1 tbsp. milk, whole or 2 percent
2 large eggs, lightly beaten

CHOCOLATE FROSTING

2 oz. unsweetened chocolate, coarsely chopped
1 oz. bittersweet chocolate, coarsely chopped
3 tbsp. unsalted butter, softened to room temperature
2¾ cups confectioners' sugar, sifted
¼ tsp. salt
1 tsp. pure vanilla extract
4 tbsp. or more milk, whole or 2 percent

Heat oven to 350 degrees. Grease a 13x9" baking pan.

For the Brownie Base: Melt the chocolate and butter in a medium saucepan over low heat, stirring to blend. Remove pan from heat and whisk in sugar, eggs, and vanilla. Stir in flour, baking powder, and salt. Gently stir in chocolate pieces. Spread *half* of the Brownie Base into prepared pan.

For the Peanut Butter Marble Base: In a medium bowl with an electric mixer, combine peanut butter and butter. Add sugar and flour, blending well. Mix in vanilla, milk, and eggs—blending until smooth. Spread Peanut Butter Marble Base over Brownie Base. Spoon remaining Brownie Base evenly over Peanut Butter Marble Base. Pull a knife through the layers in a zigzag motion to create marbling. Bake for 35 to 45 minutes or until a cake tester or toothpick inserted near the center comes out with a few moist crumbs attached. Cool pan completely on a wire rack.

For the Chocolate Frosting: Melt chocolates and butter in a medium saucepan over *low* heat, stirring often until mixture is combined. Remove saucepan from heat. Whisk in sugar, salt, vanilla, and enough milk to make a soft, spreadable frosting. Frost cooled brownies. Cut into bars. Makes about 2½ dozen.

Brownie Wedgies

Here is wedge-shaped, caramel-topped brownie enjoyment. The next time someone threatens to give you a wedgie, just smile and think of these!

BROWNIE BASE

3 oz. bittersweet chocolate, coarsely chopped

½ cup unsalted butter, softened to room temperature

¾ cup unbleached, all-purpose flour

½ cup granulated sugar

¼ cup firmly packed light brown sugar

2 tsp. pure vanilla extract

2 large eggs, lightly beaten

½ cup coarsely chopped walnuts, toasted

WEDGIE TOPPING

¼ cup In a Hurry Caramel Sauce (see index) or All the Time in the World Caramel Sauce (see index)

1 oz. unsweetened chocolate, coarsely chopped

2 tsp. unsalted butter, softened to room temperature

1 tsp. brown rice syrup or light corn syrup

Heat oven to 325 degrees. Line a 9" round cake pan with foil, extending up and beyond the sides of the pan. Grease foil.

For the Brownie Base: Melt the chocolate in a double boiler set over simmering water. Stir often, over low heat, until chocolate is melted and smooth.

Remove top of double boiler from heat, and carefully wipe bottom (so none of the moisture steams up into the chocolate); cool slightly. Whisk in butter, flour, sugars, vanilla, and eggs to blend. Spread into prepared pan. Top with nuts. Bake for 20 to 25 minutes or until a cake tester or toothpick inserted near the center comes out with a few moist crumbs attached.

For the Wedgie Topping: Warm caramel, stirring frequently, in a small saucepan until pourable. In same or another small saucepan (in case you actually *enjoy* washing multiple dishes!), melt and combine chocolate, butter, and syrup. Remove Brownie Base from pan and carefully remove foil. Drizzle caramel over Brownie Base. Drizzle chocolate mixture over caramel. Cool completely on a wire rack. Cut into wedges. Makes 12.

Brownies with Almond Crunch Topping

This cakelike confection with a crunchy, toasted-almond topping takes brownie munching to a whole new level.

BROWNIE BASE
¼ cup unsalted butter
⅔ cup granulated sugar
¼ cup unsweetened cocoa powder, sifted
1 large egg white
½ tsp. pure vanilla extract
¾ cup unbleached, all-purpose flour
⅓ cup milk, 2 percent or skim
¼ tsp. baking powder
¼ tsp. baking soda
⅓ cup chopped almonds
1 tsp. confectioners' sugar, sifted

ALMOND CRUNCH TOPPING
1½ cups finely chopped almonds, toasted
4 tbsp. light brown sugar
1 tsp. cinnamon
2 to 4 tbsp. unsalted butter, melted

Heat oven to 350 degrees. Lightly grease a 9" square pan.

For the Brownie Base: Melt the butter in a medium saucepan. Remove from heat. Whisk in sugar and cocoa powder to blend.

Add in egg white and vanilla *just until* mixture is combined. Whisk in flour, milk, baking powder, and baking soda, beating until well combined. Toss almonds with confectioners' sugar in a small bowl, then gently stir into batter. Spread into prepared pan.

For the Almond Crunch Topping: Combine all the ingredients in a small bowl until mixture is crumbly. Sprinkle evenly atop Brownie Base.

Bake for 20 to 22 minutes or until a cake tester or toothpick inserted near the center comes out clean. Cool pan completely on a wire rack. Cut into bars. Makes about 2 dozen.

Chocolate-Cheesecake-Crowned Brownies

This chocolaty, cheesecake-crowned brownie is delightful with or without toasted walnuts in the Brownie Base.

BROWNIE BASE
½ cup unsalted butter
2 oz. unsweetened chocolate, coarsely chopped
1 cup granulated sugar
1 tsp. pure vanilla extract
2 large eggs, lightly beaten
⅔ cup unbleached, all-purpose flour
½ tsp. baking powder
¼ tsp. salt

CHOCOLATE-CHEESECAKE CROWN
3 oz. semisweet chocolate, coarsely chopped
6 oz. cream cheese, softened to room temperature
1 large egg
¼ cup granulated sugar
1 tbsp. milk, whole or 2 percent
½ tsp. pure vanilla extract

Heat oven to 350 degrees. Grease and lightly flour an 8" square pan.

For the Brownie Base: Melt the butter and chocolate in a medium saucepan over low heat, stirring constantly. Remove from heat; cool slightly. Whisk in sugar and vanilla. Blend in eggs.

Whisk in flour, baking powder, and salt until blended. Spread into prepared pan. Bake for 20 to 25 minutes or until a cake tester or toothpick inserted in the center comes out with a few moist crumbs attached. Cool pan completely on a wire rack. Keep oven on.

For the Chocolate-Cheesecake Crown: Melt chocolate in a small saucepan; remove from heat and cool slightly. In a medium mixing bowl with an electric mixer, beat cream cheese with chocolate, egg, sugar, milk, and vanilla until well combined.

Spread crown over Brownie Base. Place pan in oven and bake for 10 minutes or until crown appears set. Cool pan completely on a wire rack. Chill at least 2 hours. When ready to enjoy, cut into squares. Makes about 1½ dozen.

BEV'S BITES ———

My Brownie Base is Saucepan Brownies (see index) with nuts omitted.

Leftovers? Store tightly covered (to keep others from knowing what they are!) in the refrigerator.

Chubby Cheesecake Brownies

Dedicated to my lifelong friend, Ginny, who helped me create a Chubby Cheesecake character, these are destined to become one of her favorites (and yours, too!).

BROWNIE BASE
4 oz. bittersweet chocolate, coarsely chopped
3 tbsp. unsalted butter, softened to room temperature
½ cup granulated sugar
1 tsp. pure vanilla extract
2 large eggs, lightly beaten
½ cup unbleached, all-purpose flour
½ tsp. baking powder
¼ tsp. salt

CHUBBY CHEESECAKE TOPPING
9 oz. cream cheese, softened to room temperature
½ cup granulated sugar
1 tsp. pure vanilla extract
2 large eggs, lightly beaten

CHOCOLATY GLAZE
2 oz. semisweet chocolate, coarsely chopped
1 tbsp. unsalted butter

Heat oven to 350 degrees. Lightly grease and flour a 9" square pan, being sure to tap out excess flour.

For the Brownie Base: Melt the chocolate in a double boiler set over simmering water. Stir often, over low heat, until melted and smooth.

Remove top of double boiler from heat, and carefully wipe bottom (so none of the moisture steams up into the chocolate); cool. When cool, whisk in butter, sugar, and vanilla to blend. Whisk in eggs to blend. Stir in flour, baking powder, and salt until well combined. Spread into prepared pan.

For the Chubby Cheesecake Topping: In a medium bowl with an electric mixer, combine all ingredients on medium low speed. Gently pour over Brownie Base.

Bake for 45 to 50 minutes or until a cake tester or toothpick inserted near the center comes out with a few moist crumbs attached. Cool pan completely on a wire rack.

For the Chocolaty Glaze: Melt ingredients in a small saucepan, stirring until smooth. Drizzle over brownies; refrigerate. Allow topping and glaze to set. When ready to enjoy, cut into bars. Makes about 2 dozen.

BEV'S BITE
Leftovers? Store tightly covered in the refrigerator.

Chocolate-Chip-Cookie Brownie Bars

This is what happens when two favorites collide—spoonfuls of chocolate-chip cookie dough atop a fudgy brownie layer! I was experimenting in the kitchen one day and, like a madwoman who wants to enjoy two flavors at once, I arrived at this tasty concoction. Move over, Mrs. Fields, we're munchin' through. . . .

BROWNIE BASE

4 oz. unsweetened chocolate, coarsely chopped
⅔ cup unsalted butter
2 cups granulated sugar
4 large eggs, lightly beaten
1 tsp. pure vanilla extract
1¼ cups unbleached, all-purpose flour
1 tsp. baking powder
1 tsp. salt

CHOCOLATE-CHIP COOKIE DOUGH TOPPING

¾ cup unsalted butter, melted
¾ cup firmly packed light brown sugar
½ cup granulated sugar
2 large eggs, lightly beaten
1 tsp. pure vanilla extract
1¾ cups unbleached, all-purpose flour
¾ tsp. baking soda
½ tsp. salt
1½ cups mini semisweet chocolate chips

BEV'S BITE ———

My Brownie Base is Plain and Simple Fudgy Brownies (see index) with nuts omitted.

Heat oven to 350 degrees. Lightly grease a 13x9" baking pan. Line with foil, then lightly (and gently so as not to tear it) grease foil.

For the Brownie Base: Melt the chocolate and butter in a medium saucepan over low heat, stirring to blend. Remove pan from heat and whisk in sugar, eggs, and vanilla.

Stir in flour, baking powder, and salt. Spread into prepared pan.

For the Chocolate-Chip Cookie Dough Topping: In a large bowl with an electric mixer, beat on high speed the butter and sugars until light and fluffy. Add eggs and vanilla and beat until creamy.

On low speed, blend in flour, baking soda, and salt. Stir in chocolate chips. Top Brownie Base with spoonfuls of Cookie Dough Topping, spreading gently to form an even layer (more or less).

Bake for 60 to 70 minutes or until a cake tester or toothpick inserted in the center comes out with a few moist crumbs attached. Cool pan completely on a wire rack. When completely cool, invert onto a wooden cutting board and gently remove foil. Cut into bars. Makes about 3 dozen.

Coconut-Cluster Brownies

Remember those Mounds bars you loved so much as a kid? This chewy brownie topped with coconut clusters will bring back memories (or start new ones).

BROWNIE BASE
2 cups granulated sugar
1 cup unsalted butter, softened to room temperature
1½ tsp. pure vanilla extract
4 large eggs, lightly beaten
1½ cups unbleached, all-purpose flour
⅔ cup unsweetened cocoa powder, sifted

COCONUT-CLUSTER TOPPING
2 cups sweetened toasted coconut
1 cup half-and-half
¼ cup superfine sugar

A coconut is a tough nut to crack . . . but placed atop a Brownie Base, it's easy to swallow!

Heat oven to 350 degrees. Lightly grease a 15x10x1" baking pan.

For the Brownie Base: In a medium bowl with an electric mixer, beat together the sugar and butter until light and fluffy. Add vanilla and eggs, blending well.

Add flour and cocoa; mix well. Spread into prepared pan.

For the Coconut-Cluster Topping: Combine ingredients in a small bowl. Spread over batter. Bake for 25 to 30 minutes or until a cake tester or toothpick inserted near the center comes out with a few moist crumbs attached. (Topping will be golden.) Cool pan completely on a wire rack. Cut into bars. Makes about 3½ dozen.

Coconut-Almond-Topped Brownies

This blend of flavors and textures is pure brownie almond joy!

BROWNIE BASE

2 oz. unsweetened chocolate, coarsely
   chopped
⅔ cup unbleached, all-purpose flour
½ tsp. baking powder
¼ tsp. salt
2 large eggs, lightly beaten
1 cup granulated sugar
½ cup unsalted butter, softened to
   room temperature
1 tsp. pure vanilla extract

COCONUT-ALMOND TOPPING

⅓ cup sweetened toasted coconut
¼ tsp. pure almond extract
2 oz. unsweetened chocolate, coarsely
   chopped
2 oz. semisweet chocolate, coarsely
   chopped
1 tbsp. unsalted butter, softened to
   room temperature

BEV'S BITE

My Brownie Base is Saucepan Brownies
(see index) with nuts omitted and the base
mixed *without* chocolate.

Heat oven to 350 degrees. Lightly grease an 8" square pan.

For the Brownie Base: Melt the chocolate in a double boiler set over simmering water. Stir often, over low heat, until chocolate is melted and smooth.

Remove top of double boiler from heat, and carefully wipe bottom (so none of the moisture steams up into the chocolate); set aside.

Whisk flour, baking powder, and salt in a small bowl to blend. In a large bowl with an electric mixer, beat eggs and sugar until light and blended. Blend in butter and vanilla, then stir in the flour mixture.

For the Coconut-Almond Topping: Transfer ½ *cup* Brownie Base into a small bowl. Stir in coconut and almond extract and set aside.

Add the melted unsweetened chocolate to the *remaining* Brownie Base in a large bowl. Spread into prepared pan.

Drop topping by teaspoonfuls over chocolate batter. Spread carefully to form a thin layer. Bake for 30 to 35 minutes or until a cake tester or toothpick inserted near the center comes out with a few moist crumbs attached. (Topping will be golden.) Cool pan completely on a wire rack.

Melt chocolates and butter in a small saucepan over low heat; drizzle over brownies. Cool until firm. Cut into bars. Makes about 16 to 24.

German Chocolate Brownies

These are just like a German chocolate cake but with a lot less fuss!

BROWNIE BASE

4 oz. unsweetened chocolate, coarsely chopped
⅔ cup unsalted butter
2 cups granulated sugar
4 large eggs, lightly beaten
1 tsp. pure vanilla extract
1¼ cups unbleached, all-purpose flour
1 tsp. baking powder
1 tsp. salt
1 cup sweetened coconut, toasted

FROSTING

1 cup sweet baking chocolate or milk chocolate, coarsely chopped
4 tbsp. or more milk, whole or 2 percent
½ cup confectioners' sugar, sifted
2 tbsp. unsalted butter, softened to room temperature
1 tsp. pure vanilla extract

Heat oven to 350 degrees. Butter or grease a 13x9" baking pan.

For the Brownie Base: Melt the chocolate and butter in a medium saucepan over low heat, stirring to blend. Remove pan from heat and whisk in sugar, eggs, and vanilla.

Stir in flour, baking powder, salt, and coconut. Spread into prepared pan. Bake for 25 minutes or until the brownies *just* begin to pull away from the sides of the pan. Brownies will be dry if overbaked!

For the Frosting: Melt chocolate in a small saucepan over *low* heat, stirring constantly until smooth. Remove from heat and whisk in 4 tbsp. milk, sugar, butter, and vanilla, blending until smooth. Add milk as necessary to bring frosting to proper consistency. Spread over Brownie Base. Refrigerate for 1 hour to set frosting, then remove from refrigerator. Cut into bars. Makes 4 dozen.

BEV'S BITES —————

To toast coconut, spread in a single layer on one large baking sheet and toast in a 350-degree oven for about 15 minutes or until golden brown. Stir occasionally during baking to toast evenly.

My Brownie Base is Plain and Simple Fudgy Brownies (see index) with nuts omitted and coconut added.

Irresistible Praline Brownies

The best filling for this recipe is All the Time in the World Caramel Sauce. Sure, it takes planning and a little time to prepare, and you might want to already have some sauce on hand in the refrigerator (you could have made it yesterday, you know—when you had all the time in the world!). But the taste is unbeatable and the rewards, well, they're simply irresistible!

CRUST
¾ cup unbleached, all-purpose flour
½ cup + 1 tbsp. firmly packed dark brown sugar
¾ cup finely chopped pecans, toasted
¼ cup unsalted butter, cold

BROWNIE BASE
4 oz. unsweetened chocolate, coarsely chopped
⅔ cup unsalted butter
2 cups granulated sugar
4 large eggs, lightly beaten
1 tsp. pure vanilla extract
1¼ cups unbleached, all-purpose flour
1 tsp. baking powder
1 tsp. salt
1 cup chopped pecans, lightly toasted

CARAMEL LAYER AND CHOCOLATE-FUDGE TOPPING
1½ cups All the Time in the World Caramel Sauce (see index)
1 oz. unsweetened chocolate, coarsely chopped
¼ cup unsalted butter, softened to room temperature
¼ cup half-and-half, room temperature
2¼ cups confectioners' sugar, sifted
¼ tsp. salt

BEV'S BITES ——————
My Brownie Base is Plain and Simply Fudgy Brownies (see index) using pecans.

Leftovers? Store, covered, in the refrigerator.

Heat oven to 350 degrees. Lightly grease a 13x9" baking pan.

For the Crust: In a food processor, pulse the flour, sugar, and pecans until combined. Cut the cold butter into pieces, add, and pulse quickly just until coarse crumbs form. Remove from processor bowl (I didn't really have to tell you that, did I?!) and press evenly onto bottom of prepared pan.

For the Brownie Base: Melt the chocolate and butter in a medium saucepan over low heat, stirring to blend. Remove pan from heat and whisk in sugar, eggs, and vanilla.

Stir in flour, baking powder, salt, and nuts. Spread into prepared pan. Bake for 25 minutes or until the brownies *just* begin to pull away from the sides of the pan. Brownies will be dry if overbaked! Cool pan completely on a wire rack.

For the Caramel Layer: Gently heat caramel in a small saucepan until pourable. When Brownie Base is cool, top with caramel—spreading gently. Cool to set up caramel (it will remain soft but slightly firm).

For the Chocolate-Fudge Topping: Melt the chocolate in a double boiler set over simmering water. Stir often, over low heat, until chocolate is melted and smooth.

Remove top of double boiler from heat, and carefully wipe bottom (so none of the moisture steams up into the chocolate). Transfer chocolate to a medium mixing bowl. Whisk in butter, half-and-half, sugar, and salt—beating until fluffy and smooth.

Spread topping over caramel. Refrigerate for 30 minutes (this is the cruelest part of all!). Cut into bars. Makes about 3½ dozen.

Layered Hazelnut Brownies

Toasted hazelnuts, melted chocolate, vanilla fondant, and a rich brownie layer—oh my!

BROWNIE BASE

2 oz. bittersweet chocolate, coarsely chopped
½ cup unsalted butter, softened to room temperature
1 cup granulated sugar
¾ cup unbleached, all-purpose flour
2 large eggs, lightly beaten
1 tsp. pure vanilla extract

FONDANT LAYER

2 cups confectioners' sugar, sifted
3 tbsp. heavy (whipping) cream, room temperature
¾ tsp. pure vanilla extract
¾ cup finely chopped hazelnuts, toasted

CHOCOLATE DRIZZLER

2 oz. semisweet chocolate, coarsely chopped
1 tsp. or more heavy (whipping) cream, room temperature

Heat oven to 350 degrees. Lightly grease an 8" square pan.

For the Brownie Base: Melt the chocolate in a double boiler set over simmering water. Stir often, over low heat, until chocolate is melted and smooth.

Remove top of double boiler from heat, and carefully wipe bottom (so none of the moisture steams up into the chocolate). Beat in butter, sugar, flour, eggs, and vanilla until well mixed. Spread into prepared pan. Bake for 25 minutes or until a cake tester or toothpick inserted near the center comes out with a few moist crumbs attached. Cool pan completely on a wire rack.

For the Fondant Layer: In a medium bowl with an electric mixer, beat the sugar, cream, and vanilla until mixture is smooth and blended (stopping to scrape bowl as necessary). Spread over brownies. Sprinkle with hazelnuts.

For the Chocolate Drizzler: Melt ingredients in a small saucepan over low heat, stirring, until smooth. Drizzle over Fondant Layer. Refrigerate at least 1 hour to allow the Fondant Layer and Drizzler to set up. They'll be ready to serve probably 1 hour and 1 minute after you put them into the refrigerator! Cut into bars. Makes 16.

BEV'S BITES

To toast hazelnuts, place them in a dry skillet over low heat, stirring or shaking pan often, until fragrant. Watch carefully so they don't burn. Cool before using in recipe.

Store any leftovers (huh?), covered, in the refrigerator.

Meringue Brownies

This recipe is from my first cookbook, No Reservations Required. *A sweet, crunchy meringue sits atop rich, chocolaty brownies! I developed this recipe for a heart-healthy cooking class; the pure chocolate extract adds richness without fat.*

BROWNIE BASE
½ cup unsalted butter
¼ cup unsweetened cocoa powder, sifted
¾ cup unbleached, all-purpose flour
1 tsp. baking powder
¾ cup granulated sugar
1 tsp. pure vanilla extract
1 tsp. pure chocolate extract
2 large egg whites, room temperature

MERINGUE TOPPING
1 large egg white, room temperature
⅛ tsp. salt
¼ cup granulated sugar
½ tsp. pure vanilla extract

Heat oven to 325 degrees. Lightly grease a 9" square pan.

For the Brownie Base: Melt the butter in a small saucepan over medium heat. Whisk in cocoa until smooth. Transfer mixture to a large mixing bowl.

Whisk in flour, baking powder, sugar, vanilla, chocolate extract, and egg whites; mix well. Spread into prepared pan.

For the Meringue Topping: Beat egg white with salt until foamy. Gradually add sugar, a little at a time, beating until stiff peaks form. Fold in vanilla.

Spoon meringue on top of batter. Gently and quickly spread meringue with a thin metal spatula. Bake for 25 minutes or until meringue is set and slightly browned. Cool pan completely on wire rack. Cut into squares. Makes about 1 dozen.

Just a fluff of meringue atop a heart-healthier version of a cocoa brownie. Enjoy, and feel good about it!

A Rocky Road Frosted Brownie in its natural habitat . . . surrounded by assorted rocks! (Warning: Rock placement may cause confusion— for your own safety, eat these brownies directly out of the pan.)

Rocky Road Frosted Brownies

Do I dare say your road won't be rocky when you frost your brownies this way?

BROWNIE BASE
¼ cup unsalted butter
⅔ cup granulated sugar
¼ cup unsweetened cocoa powder, sifted
1 large egg white
½ tsp. pure vanilla extract
¾ cup unbleached, all-purpose flour
⅓ cup milk, 2 percent or skim
¼ tsp. baking powder
¼ tsp. baking soda
⅓ cup chopped walnuts, toasted

ROCKY ROAD FROSTING
1 oz. unsweetened chocolate, coarsely chopped
2 tbsp. unsalted butter, softened to room temperature
1½ cups confectioners' sugar, sifted
4 tsp. milk, whole or 2 percent
½ cup mini marshmallows
½ cup coarsely chopped walnuts, toasted

Heat oven to 350 degrees. Lightly grease a 9" square pan.

For the Brownie Base: Melt the butter in a medium saucepan. Remove from heat, whisking in sugar and cocoa powder to blend.

Blend egg white and vanilla into mixture *just until* combined. Whisk in flour, milk, baking powder, and baking soda, beating until well combined. Gently stir in walnuts. Spread into prepared pan. Bake for 16 to 18 minutes or until a cake tester or toothpick inserted near the center comes out clean. Cool pan completely on a wire rack.

For the Rocky Road Frosting: Melt chocolate in a double boiler set over simmering water. Stir often, over low heat, until chocolate is melted and smooth.

Remove top of double boiler from heat, carefully wipe bottom (so none of the moisture steams up into the chocolate). Transfer chocolate to a medium bowl.

With an electric mixer, beat together chocolate, butter, sugar, and milk until smooth. Spread over Brownie Base.

Sprinkle with marshmallows and walnuts. Let Rocky Road Frosting set (30 minutes in the refrigerator should do the trick). Cut into squares. Makes about 2 dozen.

Poke 'n' Pour Fudge-Topped Brownies

The name says it all . . . a delicious Brownie Base with a creamy, fudgy chocolate topping. And for the kid in all of us, you get to poke holes in the Brownie Base and pour on the Fudge Poke—watching as the chocolate oozes in and anticipating that moment when it'll be cool enough not to burn the roof of your mouth and you can indulge!

BROWNIE BASE
¾ cup unsalted butter
4 oz. unsweetened chocolate, coarsely chopped
1½ cups granulated sugar
1 cup unbleached, all-purpose flour
3 large eggs, lightly beaten
2 tsp. pure vanilla extract

FUDGE POKE
1½ cups Smooth and Silky Fudge Sauce (see index)

Heat oven to 350 degrees. Lightly grease and flour a 13x9" baking pan.

For the Brownie Base: Melt the butter and chocolate in a medium saucepan over low heat, stirring until smooth. Whisk in sugar, stirring until smooth. Add flour, eggs, and vanilla, whisking to combine. Spread into prepared pan. Bake for 25 to 30 minutes or until a cake tester or toothpick inserted in the center comes out clean.

For the Fudge Poke: Heat the Smooth and Silky Fudge Sauce in a small saucepan over low heat, whisking constantly, until pourable.

Remove Brownie Base from the oven. Poke holes into the Base, every inch or so. Your finger (covered with a clean rubber glove—remember it's hot!) or the handle of a wooden spoon work well for this task. Immediately pour the Fudge Poke over the Brownie Base. Cool pan completely on a wire rack. (Refrigerate for extra-fudgy flavor and texture!) Cut into bars. Makes about 2 dozen.

Soufflé-Topped Brownies

This dense brownie with a luxurious chocolate "soufflé" topping is an adaptation of a brownie I purchased at a small patisserie in Montreal, Canada.

BROWNIE BASE
4 oz. semisweet chocolate, coarsely
    chopped
½ cup + 2 tbsp. unsalted butter
1 cup granulated sugar
½ tsp. pure vanilla extract
3 large eggs, lightly beaten
½ cup unbleached, all-purpose flour

SOUFFLE TOPPING
¾ cup heavy (whipping) cream
3 oz. unsweetened chocolate, finely
    chopped
3 oz. semisweet chocolate, finely
    chopped
3 large eggs, lightly beaten
5 tbsp. superfine sugar

Heat oven to 325 degrees. Lightly grease a 9" square pan.

For the Brownie Base: Melt the chocolate and butter in a medium saucepan, stirring until blended. Remove from heat; cool slightly. In a large bowl with an electric mixer, pour the melted chocolate mixture over the sugar. Beat on low speed to blend.

Add vanilla and eggs, continuing to mix on low speed to blend. Add flour, scraping the bowl as necessary to be sure all flour is blended. Spread into prepared pan.

For the Soufflé Topping: Heat cream in a small saucepan until just beginning to simmer. Remove from heat and immediately add chocolates; let sit for 2 minutes without stirring. Whisk to blend well.

In a large bowl with an electric mixer, beat eggs and sugar on high speed until mixture is pale yellow and foamy. Combine chocolate mixture with egg mixture; blend.

Pour the Soufflé over the Brownie Base. Bake for 40 to 45 minutes or until set. Cool pan completely on a wire rack. Do not cut before cool! Makes about 2 dozen.

Ultra-Rich Brownie Bars

Yes, that expression is true—you can never be too rich or have too many brownies!

BROWNIE BASE

4 oz. unsweetened chocolate, coarsely chopped

⅔ cup unsalted butter

2 cups granulated sugar

4 large eggs, lightly beaten

1 tsp. pure vanilla extract

1¼ cups unbleached, all-purpose flour

1 tsp. baking powder

1 tsp. salt

1 cup chopped walnuts or pecans, lightly toasted

CREAM BASE

12 oz. cream cheese, softened to room temperature

¼ cup confectioners' sugar, sifted

¼ cup granulated sugar

1 tsp. pure vanilla extract

1 large egg, lightly beaten

⅛ tsp. salt

2 cups mini marshmallows

FUDGE FROSTING

2 oz. unsweetened chocolate, coarsely chopped

⅓ cup milk, whole or 2 percent

⅓ cup unsalted butter, softened to room temperature

2 oz. cream cheese, softened to room temperature

4 cups confectioners' sugar, sifted

1 tsp. pure vanilla extract

Heat oven to 350 degrees. Lightly grease and flour a 13x9" baking pan.

For the Brownie Base: Melt the chocolate and butter in medium saucepan over low heat, stirring to blend.

Remove pan from heat and whisk in sugar, eggs, and vanilla. Stir in flour, baking powder, salt, and nuts. Spread into prepared pan.

For the Cream Base: In a medium bowl with an electric mixer, beat cream cheese, sugars, vanilla, egg, and salt on medium speed until smooth and fluffy. Carefully and *gently* spread over Brownie Base. Bake for 25 to 30 minutes or until a cake tester or toothpick inserted in the center comes out with a few moist crumbs attached.

Remove from oven and quickly sprinkle with marshmallows. Return to oven and bake for 2 more minutes. Remove from oven and set aside while you prepare Fudge Frosting.

For the Fudge Frosting: Combine chocolate and milk in a large saucepan over low heat, stirring until melted. Remove from heat and whisk in butter, cream cheese, sugar, and vanilla to blend. Pour over Brownie Base.

Chill at least 2 hours or until firm. Cut into bars. Makes about 2½ dozen.

BEV'S BITES

Lots of these recipes require a "chill until firm" stage. Do I need to suggest that you have some already baked and cooled brownie squares to tide you over? Better yet, get those thighs working and take a long walk while you're waiting. Perhaps you won't feel quite so guilty when you indulge!

My Brownie Base is Plain and Simple Fudgy Brownies (see index) and my Cream-Base is from Many Swirls Brownies (see index).

Vanilla-Cream-Topped Brownies with a Drizzle

This is perfect for those brownie moments when just one topping isn't enough!

BROWNIE BASE

3 oz. unsweetened chocolate, coarsely chopped
1 oz. bittersweet chocolate, coarsely chopped
½ cup unsalted butter
2 large eggs, lightly beaten
½ cup firmly packed light brown sugar
½ cup granulated sugar
2 tsp. pure vanilla extract
¾ cup unbleached, all-purpose flour
¼ tsp. salt
½ cup finely chopped pecans, toasted
2 oz. milk chocolate, coarsely chopped

VANILLA-CREAM TOPPING

½ cup unsalted butter, softened to room temperature
3 oz. cream cheese, softened to room temperature
1 tsp. pure vanilla extract
1 cup confectioners' sugar, sifted

DRIZZLE

2 oz. semisweet chocolate, coarsely chopped
2 tbsp. heavy (whipping) cream

Heat oven to 325 degrees. Lightly grease a 7x11" baking pan.

For the Brownie Base: Melt the unsweetened and bittersweet chocolates and butter in a small saucepan over low heat, stirring until smooth. Set aside to cool slightly.

In a large bowl with an electric mixer, beat eggs and sugars until blended. Add chocolate mixture and vanilla. Stir in flour and salt until mixed. Gently stir in pecans and chocolate pieces. Spread into prepared pan. Bake for 20 to 25 minutes or until a cake tester or toothpick inserted in the center comes out with a few moist crumbs attached. Cool pan completely on a wire rack.

For the Vanilla-Cream Topping: Beat together butter and cream cheese in a medium bowl with an electric mixer until light and fluffy. Gradually beat in vanilla and sugar. Spread over Brownie Base. Refrigerate until set.

For the Drizzle: Melt ingredients in a small saucepan over low heat, stirring until smooth. Remove from heat and set aside to cool to lukewarm.

To drizzle and dazzle 'em, I like to dip a fork into the Drizzle and make my own design on the Brownie Base. Be creative—you can do it!

Chill until you can no longer wait to eat them! Cut into bars. Makes about 16.

JUST A LITTLE FRUITY

Sure, I don't mind if you give me a wedgie . . .
a Berry Brownie Wedgie, that is.

Apricot Brownie Cheesecake Supremes

A shortbread crust, white chocolate blended into a cream-cheese filling, and a dark-chocolate glaze add new flavors to your brownie enjoyment!

SHORTBREAD CRUST
1 cup unbleached, all-purpose flour
¼ cup confectioners' sugar, sifted
½ cup unsalted butter, cold

SUPREME FILLING
6 oz. white chocolate, coarsely chopped
½ cup apricot jam
3 oz. cream cheese, softened to room temperature
2 tbsp. milk, whole, 2 percent, or skim

GLAZE
3 oz. semisweet chocolate, coarsely chopped
2 tbsp. unsalted butter

BEV'S BITE
Think about it . . . pouring a hot glaze over the filling will melt it! This is not a good thing, as it delays your brownie pleasure. So be sure to cool the glaze to room temperature.

Heat oven to 375 degrees.

For the Shortbread Crust: In a food processor, pulse the flour and sugar until combined. Cut the cold butter into pieces, add, and pulse until mixture is crumbly. Press into the bottom of an ungreased 9" square pan. Bake for 15 minutes or until a light golden brown.

For the Supreme Filling: Melt chocolate in a double boiler set over simmering water. Stir often, over low heat, until chocolate is melted and smooth.

Remove top of double boiler from heat, and carefully wipe bottom (so none of the moisture steams up into the chocolate). Set aside to cool.

Gently spread apricot jam evenly over baked crust. In a small bowl with an electric mixer, beat cream cheese and milk until smooth. Add chocolate to mixture, beating until smooth. Drop by spoonfuls evenly over jam. Gently spread to cover jam. Refrigerate about 1 hour or until set.

For the Glaze: Melt ingredients in a small saucepan over low heat, stirring until smooth. Remove from heat and cool to room temperature. Spread over Supreme Filling. Cool until firm. Cut into bars. Makes about 2 dozen.

Banana Brownies

If you topped this with ice cream, would it taste like a banana split?
Try it and see. . . .

BROWNIE BASE

3 oz. bittersweet chocolate, coarsely
   chopped
¾ cup granulated sugar
¼ cup firmly packed light brown sugar
½ cup unsalted butter, softened to
   room temperature
½ cup mashed ripe banana
3 large eggs, lightly beaten
1 cup unbleached, all-purpose flour
½ tsp. baking powder
¼ tsp. salt
1 cup chopped pecans, toasted and
   cooled

Heat oven to 350 degrees. Lightly grease a 13x9" baking pan.

For the Brownie Base: Melt the chocolate in a double boiler set over simmering water. Stir often, over low heat, until chocolate is smooth.

Remove top of double boiler from heat, and carefully wipe bottom (so none of the moisture steams up into the chocolate); cool chocolate to room temperature.

In a large bowl with an electric mixer, beat on medium-high speed the sugars, butter, chocolate, banana, and eggs until mixture is combined and smooth, stopping to scrape the bowl often.

Add flour, baking powder, and salt, mixing on low speed until well combined. Stir in pecans. Spread into prepared pan. Bake for 25 minutes or until a cake tester or toothpick inserted near the center comes out with a few moist crumbs attached. Cool pan completely on a wire rack. Cut into bars. Makes 3 dozen.

Berry Brownie Wedgies

This layered, fruit-and-cream-cheese-filled brownie is presented in something other than the "same old shape"! I like the light flavor of the Neufchatel cheese in the filling—you'll simply have to forgive the fact that it's lower in fat.

CREAM-CHEESE FILLING
8 oz. Neufchatel cheese, softened to
   room temperature
½ cup berry preserves (blueberry,
   blackberry, or strawberry are
   favorites)
1 tbsp. unbleached, all-purpose flour
1 large egg, lightly beaten

BROWNIE BASE
3 oz. bittersweet chocolate, coarsely
   chopped
½ cup unsalted butter, softened to
   room temperature
¾ cup unbleached, all-purpose flour
½ cup granulated sugar
¼ cup firmly packed light brown sugar
2 tsp. pure vanilla extract
2 large eggs, lightly beaten

BROWNIE DRIZZLER
1 oz. semisweet chocolate, coarsely
   chopped
1 oz. white chocolate, coarsely chopped
2 tbsp. unsalted butter, divided
1 to 2 tbsp. heavy (whipping) cream,
   divided

BEV'S BITES

Neufchatel is a soft cheese, similar to cream cheese, with less fat. It's a great way to get less fat and full flavor. Regular cream cheese may be substituted.

My Brownie Base is Brownie Wedgies (see index) with nuts omitted.

Heat oven to 350 degrees. Lightly grease a 9" springform pan.

For the Cream-Cheese Filling: Combine the ingredients in a small bowl. Beat with an electric mixer until blended; set aside.

For the Brownie Base: Melt chocolate in a double boiler set over simmering water. Stir often, over low heat, until chocolate is melted and smooth.

Remove top of double boiler from heat, and carefully wipe bottom (so none of the moisture steams up into the chocolate); cool slightly. Whisk in butter, flour, sugars, vanilla, and eggs until combined.

Spread *half* Brownie Base into prepared pan. Gently spread Cream-Cheese Filling over Brownie Base, then top with remaining Brownie Base, spreading evenly overfilling.

Bake for 30 to 35 minutes or until a cake tester or toothpick inserted near the center comes out with a few moist crumbs attached. Cool pan on a wire rack for 15 minutes. Gently run a butter knife around the inside edge of the springform pan to loosen. After Brownie Base is completely cooled, remove side of springform pan.

For the Brownie Drizzler: In two small saucepans, melt each chocolate with half the butter and 1½ tsp. (half a tbsp.) cream over very low heat, stirring until smooth (and adding cream as necessary to bring mixtures to thick but "drizzle" consistencies).

Drizzle each chocolate mixture, beginning with the dark chocolate and ending with the white, over the top of the Brownie Base. Allow to set for 30 minutes before cutting. Cut into wedges. Makes 1 dozen.

Bev's Date Brownies

When I was a kid, my Italian relatives were always eating dates and figs and dates and figs . . . so much so, I was sick of looking at them! Over the years I've matured (in some ways)—one of those ways being the development of these luscious date brownies.

BROWNIE BASE

¾ cup pitted dates
¼ cup brown rice syrup
2 tbsp. unsalted butter, melted
3 large eggs, lightly beaten
½ cup chocolate-flavored yogurt
1½ tsp. pure vanilla extract
2 tbsp. milk, whole or 2 percent
¾ cup unbleached, all-purpose flour
3 tbsp. unsweetened cocoa powder, sifted
¾ tsp. baking powder
1 tsp. cinnamon
½ tsp. freshly grated nutmeg
¼ tsp. salt
⅓ cup semisweet chocolate chips

BEV'S BITE

I prefer Medjool dates for this recipe. They are substantial in size with a deep red color, thick flesh, very little fiber, and a rich flavor.

Heat oven to 350 degrees. Lightly grease a 9" square pan.

For the Brownie Base: Using kitchen scissors dipped often in hot water (this helps prevent sticking), cut dates into pieces to measure more accurately.

Puree the dates in a food processor until smooth, stopping to scrape down the sides of the bowl. Add syrup, butter, eggs, yogurt, vanilla, and milk. Process again until smooth and well blended. Transfer mixture to a large bowl.

Whisk in flour, cocoa, baking powder, cinnamon, nutmeg, and salt, being sure all ingredients are combined. Stir in chocolate chips. Spread into prepared pan. Bake for 30 to 35 minutes or until a cake tester or toothpick inserted near the center comes out with a few moist crumbs attached. Cool pan completely on a wire rack. Cover with foil and allow to sit overnight. (What?!) When ready to serve (as soon as you wake up the next day?), cut into squares. Makes 1 dozen.

Fresh, Juicy Raspberry Brownies

Framboise (raspberry brandy) in the glaze and fresh raspberries atop the batter take brownies beyond an informal treat to a sophisticated dessert.

BROWNIE BASE

1 cup unsalted butter, softened to room temperature
1 cup granulated sugar
¾ cup firmly packed light brown sugar
4 large eggs, lightly beaten
½ cup unsweetened cocoa powder, sifted
1 tbsp. pure vanilla extract
1¼ cups unbleached, all-purpose flour
¼ tsp. salt
¾ pt. fresh red raspberries, cleaned and patted dry

RASPBERRY-CHOCOLATE GLAZE

4 oz. bittersweet chocolate, coarsely chopped
1 tbsp. Framboise
1 tbsp. very hot water
2 tsp. pure vanilla extract

BEV'S BITE

In order to have the proper amount of red raspberries for this recipe, buy a pint, use ¾ on the brownies, and, while they're baking, enjoy eating the rest!

Heat oven to 325 degrees. Lightly grease a 13x9" baking pan; line pan with foil, then lightly grease foil.

For the Brownie Base: In a large bowl with an electric mixer, beat the butter and sugars until light and fluffy. Add eggs, blending well.

Gently mix in cocoa, vanilla, flour, and salt. Spoon into prepared pan and smooth top. Sprinkle raspberries atop batter. Bake for 30 to 35 minutes or until a cake tester or toothpick inserted in the center comes out with a few moist crumbs attached. Cool pan completely on a wire rack.

For the Raspberry-Chocolate Glaze: Combine the ingredients in a double boiler set over barely simmering water, stirring until smooth. Remove top of double boiler and cool mixture.

Carefully and gently remove entire batch of brownies (uncut) from baking pan using foil as your "grip." Remove foil. Set wire rack over waxed paper. Place Brownie Base on wire rack. Drizzle and gently spread Raspberry-Chocolate Glaze over top and down sides of Brownie Base. Let cool until glaze sets. Cut into bars. Makes about 18.

Raspberry-Mascarpone-Filled Brownies

The flavor combination of chocolate, raspberry, and mascarpone is simply sublime. But don't just take my word for it. Start heating that oven!

BROWNIE BASE
4 oz. unsweetened chocolate, coarsely chopped
2/3 cup unsalted butter
2 cups granulated sugar
4 large eggs, lightly beaten
1 tsp. pure vanilla extract
1 1/4 cups unbleached, all-purpose flour
1 tsp. baking powder
1 tsp. salt

RASPBERRY-MASCARPONE FILLING
8 oz. mascarpone cheese, softened to room temperature
1/3 cup superfine sugar
1 large egg, lightly beaten
3/4 cup seedless red raspberry preserves

BEV'S BITES

So what is mascarpone cheese? It's a buttery, rich, double- or triple-cream cheese. It's ivory colored and has a soft, delicate flavor. It originated in Italy; however, several artisan cheese makers in the U.S. produce a luscious mascarpone. Can't find it? Use whipped cream cheese (*not* low fat!).

Leftovers? Store, tightly covered, in the refrigerator.

My Brownie Base is Plain and Simple Fudgy Brownies (see index) with nuts omitted.

Heat oven to 350 degrees. Grease and flour a 13x9" baking pan. Tap out any excess flour.

For the Brownie Base: Melt the chocolate and butter in medium saucepan over low heat, stirring to blend. Remove pan from heat and whisk in sugar, eggs, and vanilla.

Stir in flour, baking powder, and salt just until blended. Set aside.

For the Raspberry-Mascarpone Filling: In a small mixing bowl with an electric mixer, beat together mascarpone, sugar, and egg until light, fluffy, and well blended.

Pour *half* the Brownie Base into prepared pan and smooth out. Drop filling by small spoonfuls atop the Brownie Base in the pan. Spread gently to cover chocolate batter. Spoon preserves over filling.

Drop remaining Brownie Base by spoonfuls over filling. Spread chocolate batter gently and evenly so it reaches pan edges. Bake for 40 to 50 minutes or until a cake tester or toothpick inserted in the center comes out clean. Cool pan completely on a wire rack. Cut into bars. Makes about 4 dozen.

Orange Brownies

Freshly grated orange zest and OJ add that extra-special "something" to this chocolate brownie.

BROWNIE BASE
½ cup unsalted butter
2 oz. unsweetened chocolate, coarsely chopped
1 cup granulated sugar
1 tsp. pure vanilla extract
2 large eggs, lightly beaten
Finely grated zest of 1 large orange
⅔ cup unbleached, all-purpose flour
½ tsp. baking powder
¼ tsp. salt

CREAMY ORANGE FROSTING
1 cup confectioners' sugar, sifted
2 tbsp. unsalted butter, softened to room temperature
1 tbsp. juice from the zested orange
½ tsp. pure orange extract
1 additional orange

Heat oven to 350 degrees. Lightly grease and flour an 8" square pan.

For the Brownie Base: Melt the butter and chocolate in a medium saucepan over low heat, stirring constantly. Remove from heat; cool slightly. Whisk in sugar and vanilla. Blend in eggs and orange zest.

Whisk in flour, baking powder, and salt until blended. Spread into prepared pan. Bake for 20 to 25 minutes or until a cake tester or toothpick inserted in the center comes out with a few moist crumbs attached. Cool pan completely on a wire rack.

For the Creamy Orange Frosting: Combine sugar, butter, juice, and extract in a small bowl, whisking well until mixture is smooth. Frost cooled brownies. Allow frosting to set (I know, I know . . . this takes a little while!). Cut into bars. Slice the additional orange into half-slices as a garnish to serve with each bar—refreshing! Makes 2 dozen.

BEV'S BITE ——————
My Brownie Base is Saucepan Brownies (see index) with nuts omitted and orange zest added.

Orange Blondies with Chocolate Chunks

Hey, these are perfect for those blonde moments! (Oh yeah—even we nonblondes have them.) A deep, rich, butterscotch-flavored brownie with chocolate chunks . . . yum!

BROWNIE BASE
¾ cup unsalted butter
⅔ cup granulated sugar
½ cup firmly packed light brown sugar
1 large egg, lightly beaten
1 tsp. finely grated orange zest
1 tsp. Grand Marnier
2 cups unbleached, all-purpose flour
½ tsp. baking powder
¼ tsp. salt
6 oz. semisweet chocolate, coarsely chopped

Heat oven to 350 degrees. Lightly grease a 9" square pan.

For the Brownie Base: Combine the butter and sugars in a double boiler set over simmering water. Stir often, over low heat, until butter is melted and mixture is smooth.

Remove top of double boiler from heat, and carefully wipe bottom (so none of the moisture steams up into the mixture). Whisk in egg, zest, and Grand Marnier until well combined.

Gently stir in flour, baking powder, and salt. Stir in chocolate. Spread into prepared pan. Bake for 25 minutes or until a cake tester or toothpick inserted in the center comes out with a few moist crumbs attached. Cool pan completely on a wire rack. Cut into squares. Makes 2 dozen.

Tropical Brownies with Fresh (or Not!) Pineapple

Yes, pineapple and chocolate is an unusual combination, but bake, enjoy, and take a quick "trip to the tropics" with me!

BROWNIE BASE

4 oz. semisweet chocolate, coarsely chopped

1 oz. unsweetened chocolate, coarsely chopped

½ cup unsalted butter, softened to room temperature

1 cup firmly packed light brown sugar

1 tsp. pure vanilla extract

3 large eggs, lightly beaten

1 cup unbleached, all-purpose flour

½ tsp. baking powder

¼ tsp. salt

8 oz. finely chopped fresh or canned crushed pineapple (packed in its own juices)

½ cup chopped roasted macadamia nuts

½ cup confectioners' sugar, sifted

Shock your friends by serving this combo of pineapple and macadamia nuts in a moist brownie. They'll thank you for it.

Heat oven to 375 degrees.

For the Brownie Base: Combine the chocolates in a double boiler set over simmering water. Stir often, over low heat, until mixture is melted and smooth.

Remove top of double boiler from heat, and carefully wipe bottom (so none of the moisture steams up into the chocolate mixture); cool mixture to lukewarm. Whisk in butter, brown sugar, and vanilla until smooth. Whisk in eggs, beating well.

Stir in flour, baking powder, and salt just until batter is mixed. Pat the fresh pineapple dry, or drain the canned pineapple and pat dry. Remove *1¼ cups Brownie Base* to a small mixing bowl; gently stir in pineapple pieces. Add nuts to remaining Brownie Base.

Spread half the nut batter in an ungreased 9" square pan. Spoon pineapple batter evenly over nut batter. Gently spread pineapple batter to make an even layer over nut one. Spoon and spread remaining nut batter over pineapple one, spreading gently and trying to cover completely. (Don't worry if a little pineapple batter shows through—not everything is perfect in the tropics, either!)

Bake for 35 to 40 minutes or until a cake tester or toothpick inserted near the center comes out with a few moist crumbs attached. Cool pan completely on a wire rack. Dust cooled brownies with sugar. Cut into bars. Makes 2 dozen.

CHOCOLATE AND COFFEE, ANYONE?

The consummate cup in a pan! Enjoy the aromas of coffee and chocolate baking in My Favorite Cappuccino Brownies. (Could this kind of perfume be far behind?!)

Chocolate Cappuccino Brownies with Coffee Frosting

Coffeehouse aromas will permeate your house while these are baking.

BROWNIE BASE
4 oz. unsweetened chocolate, coarsely
    chopped
⅔ cup unsalted butter
2 tbsp. instant espresso powder
2 cups granulated sugar
4 large eggs, lightly beaten
1 tsp. pure vanilla extract
1 tsp. cinnamon
1¼ cups unbleached, all-purpose flour
1 tsp. baking powder
1 tsp. salt
1 cup chopped pecans, lightly toasted

COFFEE FROSTING
½ cup unsalted butter, softened to
    room temperature
2 cups confectioners' sugar, sifted
½ tsp. instant espresso powder
½ tsp. pure vanilla extract
1 tbsp. or more espresso, brewed

Heat oven to 375 degrees. Grease a 13x9" baking pan.

For the Brownie Base: Melt the chocolate and butter in a medium saucepan over low heat, stirring to blend.

Remove pan from heat. With an electric mixer, beat in espresso powder, sugar, eggs, and vanilla on medium-high speed until sugar is dissolved.

Beat in cinnamon, flour, baking powder, salt, and nuts just until mixture is combined and smooth. Spread into prepared pan. Bake for 25 minutes or until a cake tester or toothpick inserted near the center comes out with a few moist crumbs attached. Cool pan completely on a wire rack.

For the Coffee Frosting: In a small bowl, beat butter with an electric mixer until light and fluffy. Add sugar, espresso powder, vanilla, and brewed espresso, beating until smooth. Frost cooled brownies. Cut into bars. Makes 3 dozen.

BEV'S BITES ————
Serve these to friends with your favorite espresso drinks!

My Brownie Base is Plain and Simple Fudgy Brownies (see index) with additions.

My Favorite Cappuccino Brownies

A retired pastry-chef friend of mine adapted this recipe years ago from one she created for her restaurant. It's absolutely irresistible! And she has been kind enough to let me share it with my students and on TV appearances.

BROWNIE BASE
6 tbsp. unsalted butter
4½ oz. semisweet or bittersweet chocolate, coarsely chopped
1 tbsp. instant espresso powder, dissolved in 1 tbsp. pure chocolate extract or vanilla extract
¾ cup granulated sugar
1 tsp. pure vanilla extract (if not using with espresso powder)
2 large eggs, lightly beaten
½ cup unbleached, all-purpose flour
¼ tsp. salt
½ cup coarsely chopped walnuts, toasted

FROSTING
4 oz. Neufchatel cheese, softened to room temperature
4 tbsp. unsalted butter, softened to room temperature
¾ cup confectioners' sugar, sifted
1 tsp. pure vanilla extract
¾ tsp. cinnamon

PIECE DE RESISTANCE
2 tsp. instant espresso powder
1 tbsp. pure vanilla extract
4 oz. semisweet or bittersweet chocolate, coarsely chopped
1 tbsp. unsalted butter
¼ cup half-and-half

Heat oven to 350 degrees. Lightly grease an 8″ square pan.

For the Brownie Base: Combine the butter, chocolate, and dissolved espresso powder in a double boiler set over simmering water. Stir often, over low heat, until mixture is melted and smooth.

Remove top of double boiler from heat, and carefully wipe bottom (so none of the moisture steams up into the chocolate mixture). Transfer to a large bowl and cool slightly.

On low speed, beat in sugar and vanilla (if using). Add eggs, beating until smooth and well blended. Add in flour and salt just until mixture is combined. Stir in nuts. Spread into prepared pan. Bake for 25 minutes or until a cake tester or toothpick inserted near the center comes out with a few moist crumbs attached. Cool pan completely on a wire rack.

For the Frosting: In a large bowl with an electric mixer, beat cream cheese and butter until fluffy. Add sugar, vanilla, and cinnamon; beat until well combined, scraping sides of bowl often to be sure all is blended. Frost cooled brownies. Allow to set, refrigerated, for 1 hour.

For the Pièce de Résistance: In a small bowl, dissolve espresso powder in vanilla; set aside. Combine chocolate, butter, and half-and-half in a small saucepan. Set the saucepan over low heat and stir constantly, until mixture is smooth. Remove from heat. Add dissolved espresso powder, whisking to combine. Cool to room temperature. Spread over Frosting (being careful not to break down Frosting). Return brownies to the refrigerator and chill several hours. (This is most maddening, as you have to *wait* to enjoy the rich chocolate and coffee flavors of this brownie!) Cut into squares. Remove the brownies from the pan while they're still cold. Makes 2 dozen.

My Favorite Cappuccino Brownies, Variation

Here's a version that's not quite as dramatic or time consuming as the original, but delicious anyway!

BROWNIE BASE
6 tbsp. unsalted butter

4½ oz. semisweet or bittersweet chocolate, coarsely chopped

1 tbsp. instant espresso powder, dissolved in 1 tbsp. pure chocolate extract or vanilla extract

¾ cup granulated sugar

1 tsp. pure vanilla extract (if not using with espresso powder)

2 large eggs, lightly beaten

½ cup unbleached, all-purpose flour

¼ tsp. salt

½ cup coarsely chopped pecans, toasted

MOCHA CREAM
1 cup heavy (whipping) cream, cold

4 tbsp. confectioners' sugar, sifted

2 tsp. unsweetened cocoa powder, sifted

1 tsp. pure vanilla extract

2 tsp. instant espresso powder dissolved in 2 tsp. hot water, then cooled

Heat oven to 350 degrees. Lightly grease an 8" square pan.

For the Brownie Base: Combine the butter, chocolate, and dissolved espresso powder in a double boiler set over simmering water. Stir often, over low heat, until mixture is melted and smooth.

Remove top of double boiler from heat, and carefully wipe bottom (so none of the moisture steams up into the chocolate mixture). Transfer to a large bowl and cool slightly.

On low speed, beat in sugar and vanilla (if using). Add eggs, beating until smooth and well blended. Add in flour and salt just until mixture is combined. Stir in nuts. Spread into prepared pan. Bake for 25 minutes or until a cake tester or toothpick inserted near the center comes out with a few moist crumbs attached. Cool pan completely on a wire rack.

For the Mocha Cream: In a large (*cold*) bowl with an electric mixer, beat ingredients until soft peaks form.

Cut Brownie Base into squares. Top each with a generous dollop (isn't this a fun word?!) of the Mocha Cream. Makes 2 dozen.

Orange Cappuccino Brownies

The infusion of fresh orange flavor and espresso powder is divine!
Serve this for dessert when company's coming.

BROWNIE BASE
4 oz. unsweetened chocolate, coarsely
   chopped
⅔ cup unsalted butter
2 cups granulated sugar
4 large eggs, lightly beaten
1 tsp. Grand Marnier
1¼ cups unbleached, all-purpose flour
1 tsp. baking powder
1 tsp. salt
1 tsp. finely grated orange zest
1 tsp. instant espresso powder

FROSTING
Milk Chocolate Frosting (see index)

GLAZE
¼ cup confectioners' sugar, sifted
½ tsp. finely grated orange zest
1 to 2 tsp. Grand Marnier

Heat oven to 350 degrees. Lightly grease a 13x9" baking pan.

For the Brownie Base: Melt the chocolate and butter in a medium saucepan over low heat, stirring to blend.

Remove pan from heat. Whisk in sugar, eggs, and Grand Marnier.

Stir in flour, baking powder, salt, orange zest, and espresso powder. Spread into prepared pan. Bake for 25 minutes or until the brownies *just* begin to pull away from the sides of the pan. Brownies will be dry if overbaked! Cool pan completely on a wire rack.

For the Frosting: Frost cooled brownies.

For the Glaze: Whisk together ingredients in a small bowl until smooth, using enough of the Grand Marnier for a glaze consistency. Drizzle over Frosting. Cut into bars. Makes about 3 dozen.

*If your local coffee shop served this brownie bar, you'd skip the
coffee and get a cup of these instead.*

Espresso Cheesecake Brownie Bars

Chocolate cookie crumbs and a cheesecake layer shine in this decadent bar!

BROWNIE BASE
½ cup unsalted butter
3 oz. unsweetened chocolate, coarsely chopped
1 cup firmly packed light brown sugar
½ tsp. pure vanilla extract
2 large eggs, lightly beaten
½ cup unbleached, all-purpose flour
¼ cup mini semisweet chocolate chips

ESPRESSO LAYER
1½ cups chocolate cookie crumbs
1 tsp. instant espresso powder
¼ cup unsalted butter, melted
8 oz. cream cheese, softened to room temperature
¼ cup granulated sugar
½ tsp. pure vanilla extract
1 large egg, lightly beaten

BEV'S BITES ——————
To make chocolate cookie crumbs, buy those plain chocolate cookies (Nabisco and Newman's Own are two available brands) and "crumb them up" in your processor or in a Ziploc plastic bag (sealed, of course), using a rolling pin to smash.

My Brownie Base is Fudge Brownies (see index).

Heat oven to 350 degrees. Lightly grease an 8" square pan.

For the Brownie Base: Melt the butter and chocolate in a large saucepan over low heat, stirring until smooth.

Remove saucepan from heat. Using an electric mixer, beat in sugar and vanilla. Add eggs, beating well.

Stir in flour, mixing until batter is smooth. Gently stir in chips. Spread into prepared pan.

For the Espresso Layer: Combine cookie crumbs, espresso powder, and butter in a medium bowl, mixing well. Reserve ⅓ *cup* of the mixture for the bar topping. Sprinkle remaining mixture atop Brownie Base.

In a medium bowl with an electric mixer, beat the cream cheese until smooth. Blend in the sugar, vanilla, and egg. Drop by spoonfuls over crumb mixture, smoothing gently, then sprinkle with remaining crumb mixture. Bake for 25 minutes or until a cake tester or toothpick inserted near the center comes out with a few moist crumbs attached. Cool pan completely on a wire rack.

Refrigerate until firm (sorry for the wait!). Cut into bars. Makes about 2 dozen.

(More Than Double) Espresso Brownies

Enjoy the "jolt" of dark, strong, finely ground Italian coffee in this fun version of coffee and chocolate.

BROWNIE BASE
4 oz. unsweetened chocolate, coarsely chopped
⅔ cup unsalted butter
2 cups granulated sugar
4 large eggs, lightly beaten
1 tsp. pure vanilla extract
1¼ cups unbleached, all-purpose flour
1 tsp. baking powder
1 tsp. salt
2 tsp. instant espresso powder
1 cup chopped walnuts or pecans, lightly toasted

CHOCOLATE FILLING
¼ cup + 2 tbsp. unsalted butter, softened to room temperature
¾ cup firmly packed light brown sugar
1 large egg, lightly beaten
2 tsp. instant espresso powder
12 oz. bittersweet chocolate, coarsely chopped

ESPRESSO GLAZE
4 oz. semisweet or bittersweet chocolate, coarsely chopped
1 tbsp. unsalted butter
¼ tsp. instant espresso powder
1 to 2 tsp. heavy (whipping) cream or half-and-half

Heat oven to 350 degrees. Lightly grease a 13x9" baking pan.

For the Brownie Base: Melt the chocolate and butter in a medium saucepan over low heat, stirring to blend.

Remove pan from heat. Whisk in sugar, eggs, and vanilla. Stir in flour, baking powder, salt, espresso powder, and nuts. Spread into prepared pan. Bake for 20 minutes. Cool slightly.

For the Chocolate Filling: Beat butter and sugar in a small bowl with an electric mixer until light and fluffy. Add egg and espresso powder, blending well. Gently fold in chocolate.

Gently spoon and spread Chocolate Filling over the Brownie Base. Bake for 15 to 20 additional minutes or until light golden brown.

For the Espresso Glaze: Melt chocolate and butter in a small saucepan over low heat, stirring until smooth. Remove from heat and whisk in espresso powder and cream until desired consistency is reached. Drizzle over warm brownies. Cool pan completely on a wire rack. Cut into bars. Makes about 3 dozen.

BEV'S BITE ————
My Brownie Base is Plain and Simple Fudgy Brownies (see index) with the addition of instant espresso powder.

Kahlua Brownies, Anyone?

Rich, decadent brownies . . . have a brownie party and be sure to include these adult treats!

BROWNIE BASE
4 oz. unsweetened chocolate, coarsely
    chopped
²⁄₃ cup unsalted butter
2 cups granulated sugar
4 large eggs, lightly beaten
1 tbsp. Kahlua
1¼ cups unbleached, all-purpose flour
1 tsp. baking powder
1 tsp. salt
1 cup chopped walnuts or pecans,
    lightly toasted

FROSTING
1 tsp. instant espresso powder
2½ tbsp. Kahlua, divided
½ cup unsalted butter, softened to
    room temperature
2 cups confectioners' sugar, sifted
2 to 3 tsp. half-and-half or heavy
    (whipping) cream

Heat oven to 350 degrees. Lightly grease a 13x9" baking pan.

For the Brownie Base: Melt the chocolate and butter in a medium saucepan over low heat, stirring to blend.

Remove pan from heat. Whisk in sugar, eggs, and Kahlua.

Stir in flour, baking powder, salt, and nuts. Spread into prepared pan. Bake for 25 minutes or until the brownies *just* begin to pull away from the sides of the pan. Brownies will be dry if overbaked! Cool pan completely on a wire rack.

For the Frosting: Dissolve espresso powder in 1½ tbsp. Kahlua. Cream butter until fluffy in a medium bowl with an electric mixer. On low speed, blend in sugar, espresso mixture, and remaining Kahlua. Add enough half-and-half or cream for a smooth spreadable frosting. Frost cooled brownies. Allow to set, refrigerated, for 30 minutes. Cut into bars. Makes about 3½ dozen.

BEV'S BITE ───────────
My Brownie Base is Plain and Simple Fudgy Brownies (see index) with vanilla omitted and Kahlua added.

Fudge-Frosted Coffee and Almond Brownies

Almond pairs so well with chocolate and coffee, you'll wonder why you didn't try this combination sooner. This fudge frosting has been a family recipe since as long as I can remember licking the bowl.

BROWNIE BASE
5 oz. semisweet chocolate, coarsely chopped
½ cup unsalted butter, softened to room temperature
4 large eggs, separated
1 cup superfine sugar
1 cup finely chopped almonds
1 cup unbleached, all-purpose flour
2 tbsp. espresso, brewed
1 tsp. pure almond extract

BEV'S FUDGE FROSTING
¼ cup granulated sugar
¼ cup firmly packed light brown sugar
¼ cup heavy (whipping) cream
2 tbsp. unsalted butter, softened to room temperature
2½ oz. semisweet chocolate, coarsely chopped
1 cup confectioners' sugar, sifted
½ tsp. pure vanilla extract

Heat oven to 350 degrees. Lightly grease a 13x9" baking pan.

For the Brownie Base: Melt the chocolate in a double boiler set over simmering water. Stir often, over low heat, until chocolate is smooth.

Remove top of double boiler from heat, and carefully wipe bottom (so none of the moisture steams up into the chocolate). Whisk in butter until blended and smooth.

In a medium bowl, beat room-temperature egg whites with an electric mixer until soft peaks form. Continue beating, adding sugar a tablespoonful at a time, until stiff peaks form. Fold in almonds.

In a large bowl, mix flour, espresso, melted chocolate, egg yolks (lightly beaten), and almond extract, blending well.

Gently fold in egg-white mixture. Spread into prepared pan. Bake for 25 to 35 minutes or until a cake tester or toothpick inserted near the center comes out with a few moist crumbs attached. Cool pan completely on a wire rack.

For Bev's Fudge Frosting: Combine the granulated and brown sugars, cream, butter, and chocolate in a saucepan. Boil, stirring constantly. Reduce heat; simmer and stir until mixture is melted and smooth. Remove saucepan from heat. Whisk in confectioners' sugar and vanilla until smooth. Frost cooled brownies. Chill for 1 hour to firm. Cut into bars. Makes 3 dozen.

Definitely a "sit back, put your feet up, and savor every bite" brownie!

Super-Simple Mocha Brownies

Deep chocolate flavor and a hint of coffee . . . these brownies are definitely super simple. Don't skimp on ingredients. Better-quality chocolates will give them a noticeably richer flavor.

BROWNIE BASE
2 oz. bittersweet chocolate, coarsely chopped
2 oz. unsweetened chocolate, coarsely chopped
5 tbsp. unsalted butter
1 cup granulated sugar
2 tsp. instant espresso powder
2 large eggs, lightly beaten
¼ cup milk, whole or 2 percent
1½ tsp. pure vanilla extract
½ cup unbleached, all-purpose flour
½ tsp. baking powder
¼ tsp. salt

Heat oven to 350 degrees. Lightly grease and flour an 8" square pan.

For the Brownie Base: Combine the chocolates in a double boiler set over simmering water. Stir often, over low heat, until mixture is melted and smooth.

Remove top of double boiler from heat, and carefully wipe bottom (so none of the moisture steams up into the chocolate mixture). Transfer chocolate mixture to a medium bowl; cool slightly.

Whisk in butter, sugar, and espresso powder. Beat in eggs, blending well. Whisk in milk and vanilla. Add in flour, baking powder, and salt just until mixture is combined. Spread into prepared pan. Bake for 25 minutes or until a cake tester or toothpick inserted in the center comes out with a few moist crumbs attached. Cool pan completely on a wire rack. Cut into squares. Makes 9 (if you're hungry) or 1 dozen.

Mocha Brownie Wedgie Sundae

This delightful mocha brownie wedge is topped with ice cream and a silky smooth fudge sauce.

BROWNIE BASE
1 tsp. instant espresso powder
1 tbsp. milk
½ cup unsalted butter
2 oz. unsweetened chocolate, coarsely chopped
1 cup granulated sugar
1 tsp. pure vanilla extract
2 large eggs, lightly beaten
⅔ cup unbleached, all-purpose flour

SUNDAE TOPPINGS
½ gal. coffee ice cream
1 cup walnut pieces, toasted
Smooth and Silky Fudge Sauce (see index)

Heat oven to 350 degrees. Lightly grease a pizza pan (12 to 13" size).

For the Brownie Base: In a small saucepan over low heat, stir the espresso powder into the milk until mixture is warm and well combined. Set aside.

Melt butter and chocolate in a medium saucepan over low heat, stirring constantly. Remove saucepan from heat; cool slightly. Whisk in sugar, vanilla, and espresso mixture. Blend in eggs.

Whisk in flour until blended. Spread into prepared pan. Bake for 14 to 16 minutes or until a cake tester or toothpick inserted in the center comes out with a few moist crumbs attached. Cool pan completely on a wire rack.

When ready to serve, cut into wedges and top with ice cream, nuts, and Smooth and Silky Fudge Sauce. Do we dare add whipped cream and a cherry? Makes about 10.

SHAKE 'EM UP

The grand prize for knowing that hazelnuts are also called filberts or cobnuts is two pieces of this decadent, crunchy favorite, Chocolate-Hazelnut Truffle Brownies.

Chipotle Brownies

Why chipotle chiles (smoked jalapeño peppers) in brownies? Why not? Chipotles intensify the chocolate flavor and add a tiny kick of mysterious heat.

BROWNIE BASE
¼ cup unsalted butter + more for pan
3 oz. bittersweet chocolate, coarsely
    chopped
⅓ cup granulated sugar
1 tsp. finely chopped canned chipotle
    chiles
1 tsp. adobo sauce from chiles
1 tsp. pure vanilla extract
Pinch cayenne pepper
1 large egg, lightly beaten
⅓ cup unbleached, all-purpose flour

Heat oven to 350 degrees. Lightly grease an 8" square pan with butter.

For the Brownie Base: Cut the ¼ cup butter into pieces. Stir butter and chocolate in a medium saucepan over medium low heat until melted and combined.

Remove saucepan from heat. Quickly blend in sugar, chipotles, adobo sauce, vanilla, and cayenne. Whisk in egg, then flour, making a smooth batter. Spread into prepared pan. Bake for 20 to 25 minutes or until the brownies *just* begin to pull away from the sides of the pan (the center should be firm). Cool pan completely on a wire rack. Cut into squares. Makes 12 to 16.

BEV'S BITE ————————
Add a little cayenne pepper to one of my frosting recipes—and watch their eyes light up!

If I told you this brownie contained a hot chile with wrinkled, dark-brown skin and a smoky-sweet flavor, would you still share?

Chocolaty, Spicy Brownies

Another variation on the chile pepper and chocolate theme, these moist chocolaty brownies are warmed by the addition of cinnamon and chili powder.

BROWNIE BASE
Cocoa powder, sifted
8 oz. unsweetened chocolate, coarsely chopped
¾ cup unsalted butter
5 large eggs, lightly beaten
1¾ cups granulated sugar
1¼ cups unbleached, all-purpose flour
½ cup unsweetened cocoa powder, sifted
1 tbsp. freshly ground cinnamon
½ tsp. chili powder
¼ tsp. salt
2 tsp. pure vanilla extract
¾ cup pine nuts, toasted

BEV'S BITES ———————

You know your share of nuts, but *pine* nuts? These nuts come from several varieties of pine trees. They are grown mainly in China, Italy, Mexico, North Africa, and the southwestern part of the U.S. The Mediterranean or Italian pine nut has a light, delicate flavor; the Chinese pine nut has a stronger flavor. Because of their high fat content, they should be stored, covered, in the refrigerator or freezer.

These brownies are delicious with a mug of hot chocolate that contains a stick of cinnamon!

Heat oven to 350 degrees. Lightly grease a 13x9" baking pan. Dust pan with some cocoa powder, shaking out excess.

For the Brownie Base: Combine the chocolate and butter in a double boiler set over simmering water. Stir often, over low heat, until mixture is melted and smooth.

Remove top of double boiler from heat, and carefully wipe bottom (so none of the moisture steams up into the chocolate mixture). Set aside to cool slightly.

In a large bowl of an electric mixer, beat eggs and sugar on high speed until light and lemon colored (this takes 3 to 4 minutes). Add chocolate mixture, beating on low speed to blend. Add flour, ½ cup cocoa powder, cinnamon, chili powder, and salt, beating on low speed until combined. Stop occasionally and scrape sides of bowl and paddle.

Add vanilla and beat at medium speed until combined. Stir in pine nuts. Spread into prepared pan. Bake for 30 minutes or until a cake tester or toothpick inserted near the center comes out with a few moist crumbs attached. Cool pan completely on a wire rack. Cut into bars. Makes 2 to 3 dozen.

Brownies with Chocolate Butter

Okay, so this is pure decadence . . . and you know you can feel your thighs getting bigger just thinking about it. So, let's talk while you walk 5 miles, jog 7 miles, or cycle for 10 minutes. Eating brownies smeared with a touch of Chocolate Butter is like enjoying a fresh buttermilk biscuit with your favorite honey-butter or cinnamon-butter spread. It's not something you should have every day, but certainly worth indulging in once in awhile. I've listed below my favorite brownie selections for this treat . . . then, of course, the simple recipe for Chocolate Butter. See the index for the brownie recipes.

BROWNIE BASE OPTIONS
Plain and Simple Fudgy Brownies
Fudge Brownies
Saucepan Brownies
Old-Fashioned Brownies

CHOCOLATE BUTTER
1 oz. bittersweet chocolate, coarsely chopped
1 oz. semisweet chocolate, coarsely chopped
1 cup unsalted butter, softened to room temperature

BEV'S BITE —————
If you find yourself with leftover Chocolate Butter, you can roll it into a log shape, wrap in plastic wrap, and freeze or refrigerate for another time. It will keep for 6 months in the freezer (but not at my house!) or 1 week in the refrigerator.

For the Chocolate Butter: Combine the chocolates in a double boiler set over simmering water. Stir often, over low heat, until mixture is melted and smooth.

Remove top of double boiler from heat, and carefully wipe bottom (so none of the moisture steams up into the chocolate mixture). Transfer to a large bowl of an electric mixer. Set aside until cool to the touch.

Beat cooled chocolate with butter on medium speed until blended, stopping often to scrape sides of bowl and paddle. Beat mixture on high speed until light and fluffy. Serve with your choice of Brownie Base.

Waiter, There's a Truffle in My Brownie!

A favorite from my first cookbook, No Reservations Required, *this all-adult brownie is a version you'll soon be addicted to!*

BROWNIE BASE
½ cup unsalted butter
3 oz. bittersweet chocolate, coarsely
   chopped
2 large eggs, lightly beaten
1⅓ cups granulated sugar
1 tsp. pure vanilla extract
¾ cup unbleached, all-purpose flour
1 lb. solid-center chocolate truffles

BEV'S BITES ———————

This is a much more "fluid" brownie when done and not at all cakelike. The mixture will firm up as it cools but still maintain its chocolaty, gooey texture!

Do you dare? Top portions to taste with vanilla ice cream and a sprinkling of cocoa powder!

Heat oven to 350 degrees. Lightly grease a 9" square pan.

For the Brownie Base: Combine the butter and chocolate in a double boiler set over simmering water. Stir often, over low heat, until mixture is melted and smooth.

Remove top of double boiler from heat, and carefully wipe bottom (so none of the moisture steams up into the chocolate mixture). Transfer chocolate mixture to a medium bowl.

Whisk in eggs, sugar, and vanilla, blending well. Stir in flour until all is incorporated. Cut truffles into ½" pieces and gently stir in. Gently spoon mixture into prepared pan. Bake for about 25 minutes or until brownies appear set. Cool pan completely on a wire rack. Cut into small squares. Serve warm or cool. Makes 6.

*A crackly top and a soft, sensual "oozing with chocolate"
center . . . where's my spoon?*

Chocolate-Hazelnut Truffle Brownies

Loosely based on a brownie served at one of my favorite café/delis on the East Coast, this decadent treat puts a sophisticated spin on a brownie. Notice how little flour goes into the finished product, giving it much more of a chocolate-truffle texture.

CRUST
2 cups coarsely chopped skinned hazelnuts, toasted

BROWNIE BASE
8 oz. bittersweet chocolate, coarsely chopped
8 oz. semisweet chocolate, coarsely chopped
1 cup unsalted butter
6 large eggs, lightly beaten
1 cup granulated sugar
1/3 cup unbleached, all-purpose flour

HAZELNUT FROSTING
1 cup unsalted butter, softened to room temperature
3 cups confectioners' sugar, sifted
1 tsp. hazelnut liqueur
1 cup coarsely chopped skinned hazelnuts, toasted

BEV'S BITES
The surprise crunch at the bottom of these brownies is one of those things I can't get enough of!

Just ran out of hazelnut liqueur? Pure vanilla extract makes an acceptable substitute in this recipe.

A different brownie shape adds a touch of sophistication to any recipe. Ponder this while you're deciding how many you should or shouldn't have!

Heat oven to 350 degrees. Generously butter a 13x9" baking pan.

For the Crust: Spread the hazelnuts in the bottom of prepared pan, pressing with a metal spatula to make an even layer.

For the Brownie Base: Melt the chocolates and butter in a medium saucepan over low heat, stirring until mixture is blended and smooth. Remove saucepan from heat and set aside.

In a large bowl with an electric mixer, beat eggs and sugar at high speed, stopping and scraping the bowl often, until thick and lemon colored (this will take 3 to 4 minutes). On low speed, stir in chocolate and flour until incorporated, stopping and scraping the bowl often until thoroughly combined. Spread onto crust. Bake for 30 to 40 minutes or until a cake tester or toothpick inserted near the center comes out with a few moist crumbs attached. Cool pan completely on a wire rack.

For the Hazelnut Frosting: In a large bowl with an electric mixer, beat butter on medium high speed until light and fluffy. Add sugar, a little at a time, stopping and scraping the bowl often. Add liqueur and beat at medium speed until mixture is smooth and of a spreading consistency. Blend in nuts on low speed. Frost cooled brownies. Allow to set for 30 minutes. Cut into squares. Cut each square in half diagonally to form 2 triangular shapes. Makes about 3 1/2 dozen.

Chocolate, Chocolate, and More Chocolate Fudge Brownies

Three times is the charm in this fudge brownie that covers all the chocolate bases.

BROWNIE BASE
4½ oz. semisweet chocolate, coarsely chopped
¼ cup unsalted butter, softened to room temperature
½ cup granulated sugar
3 large eggs, lightly beaten
½ cup unbleached, all-purpose flour
3 tbsp. unsweetened cocoa powder, sifted
1 tbsp. pure vanilla extract

CHOCOLATE GLAZE
3 oz. bittersweet chocolate, coarsely chopped
2 tbsp. unsalted butter
2 tbsp. light corn syrup or brown rice syrup
1 tbsp. or more milk
⅓ cup confectioners' sugar, sifted

CHOCOLATE DRIZZLER
1½ oz. milk chocolate, coarsely chopped
1½ oz. white chocolate, coarsely chopped
2 tbsp. unsalted butter

Heat oven to 350 degrees. Lightly grease and flour a 9" square pan, tapping out any excess flour.

For the Brownie Base: Melt the chocolate in a double boiler set over simmering water. Stir often, over low heat, until chocolate is melted and smooth.

Remove top of double boiler from heat, and carefully wipe bottom (so none of the moisture steams up into the chocolate). Whisk in butter until smooth; set aside.

In a large bowl with an electric mixer, beat sugar and eggs on medium-high speed, until thick, very smooth, and light. On low speed, stir in chocolate mixture, flour, cocoa, and vanilla. Spread into prepared pan. Bake for about 25 minutes or until a cake tester or toothpick inserted near the center comes out with a few moist crumbs attached. Cool pan completely on a wire rack.

For the Chocolate Glaze: Melt chocolate and butter in a small saucepan over low heat, stirring until mixture is blended and smooth. Remove saucepan from heat. Whisk in syrup and milk. Add sugar, a third at a time, whisking after each addition until mixture is smooth and spreadable. (Add milk if needed.) Spread Chocolate Glaze over cooled Brownie Base.

For the Chocolate Drizzler: In separate small saucepans, melt chocolates over very low heat, stirring, just until smooth. Remove saucepans from heat and quickly add half the butter to each saucepan, whisking to blend.

Drizzle both chocolates (beginning with milk then white) over Chocolate Glaze. Let stand about 20 minutes to allow Glaze and Drizzler a chance to set. Cut into squares. Makes 2 dozen.

Empty the Pantry Brownies

If you love lots of "stuff" in and atop your brownies, this recipe is for you.

BROWNIE BASE
2 oz. semisweet chocolate, coarsely
  chopped
4 oz. bittersweet chocolate, coarsely
  chopped
1 cup granulated sugar
½ cup firmly packed light brown sugar
¾ cup unsalted butter
3 large eggs, lightly beaten
1 tsp. pure vanilla extract
1 tsp. pure chocolate extract
¾ cup unbleached, all-purpose flour
¼ tsp. baking soda

CARAMEL LAYERING
In a Hurry Caramel Sauce (see index)

"STUFF" ATOP
1 cup coarsely chopped hazelnuts or
  macadamia nuts, toasted
8 oz. semisweet chocolate chips
8 oz. milk chocolate chips

Heat oven to 325 degrees. Lightly grease and flour a 9" square pan.

For the Brownie Base: Combine the chocolates in a double boiler set over simmering water. Stir often, over low heat, until mixture is melted and smooth.

Remove top of double boiler from heat, and carefully wipe bottom (so none of the moisture steams up into the chocolate mixture). Set aside to cool.

In a large bowl with an electric mixer, beat sugars and butter on medium high speed until light and fluffy. Add eggs and beat until well blended. Add chocolate mixture and extracts, beating until blended. Slowly beat in flour and baking soda, stopping occasionally to scrape sides of bowl. Spread into prepared pan. Bake for 40 to 45 minutes or until a cake tester or toothpick inserted near the center comes out with a few moist crumbs attached. Cool pan completely on a wire rack.

For the Caramel Layering: Prepare sauce and set aside to cool. Spread over cooled brownies (if it appears to be too much sauce, just spread enough to evenly coat brownies and set remainder aside for another use).

For the "Stuff" Atop: Place nuts and chips over sauce on brownies. Place pan in the 325-degree oven to set things up. This will only take 6 minutes. Cool pan completely on a wire rack. Cut into squares. Makes 1 dozen.

Hidden "Candy Bar" Brownies

This is one of my favorite ways to add instant flavor and some crunch to my brownies.

BROWNIE BASE

½ cup unsalted butter
2 oz. unsweetened chocolate, coarsely chopped
1 cup granulated sugar
1 tsp. pure vanilla extract
2 large eggs, lightly beaten
⅔ cup unbleached, all-purpose flour
½ tsp. baking powder
¼ tsp. salt
6 oz. chocolate toffee candy bar, coarsely chopped

Heat oven to 350 degrees. Grease and lightly flour *bottom only* of an 8" square pan.

For the Brownie Base: Melt the butter and chocolate in a medium saucepan over low heat, stirring constantly. Remove saucepan from heat; cool slightly.

With a large spoon, blend in sugar and vanilla. Blend in eggs. Stir in flour, baking powder, and salt until blended. Gently stir in candy pieces. Spread in prepared pan. Bake for 20 to 25 minutes or until set in the center. Cool pan completely on a wire rack. Cut into squares. Makes 6.

BEV'S BITE ——————

My Brownie Base is Saucepan Brownies (see index) with nuts omitted and candy pieces added.

Mint Buttercream Brownies

These are fudgy with "a hint of mint" and a smooth buttercream . . . yum!

BROWNIE BASE
2 oz. unsweetened chocolate, coarsely chopped
½ cup unsalted butter, softened to room temperature
¾ cup granulated sugar
¾ cup unbleached, all-purpose flour
2 large eggs, lightly beaten

MINT BUTTERCREAM
2¼ cups confectioners' sugar, sifted
4 tbsp. unsalted butter, softened to room temperature
3 oz. cream cheese, softened to room temperature
¼ tsp. pure mint extract (spearmint or peppermint)

CHOCOLATE DRIZZLER
2 oz. bittersweet chocolate, coarsely chopped
1 tbsp. unsalted butter

BEV'S BITE ———————
Leftovers? Store, covered, in the refrigerator.

Heat oven to 350 degrees. Lightly grease a 9" square pan.

For the Brownie Base: Melt the chocolate in a double boiler set over simmering water. Stir often, over low heat, until chocolate is melted and smooth.

Remove top of double boiler from heat, and carefully wipe bottom (so none of the moisture steams up into the chocolate). Whisk in butter, sugar, flour, and eggs until well blended. Spread into prepared pan. Bake for 25 minutes or until a cake tester or toothpick inserted near the center comes out with a few moist crumbs attached. Cool pan completely on a wire rack.

For the Mint Buttercream: In a large bowl with an electric mixer, beat ingredients on low speed to combine. Stop and scrape sides of bowl, then continue to beat at medium speed until mixture is creamy and well combined.

For the Chocolate Drizzler: Melt ingredients in a small saucepan over low heat, stirring constantly, until mixture is smooth. Remove saucepan from heat and cool slightly.

Spread Mint Buttercream over cooled Brownie Base, and then drizzle with the Chocolate Drizzler. Cool completely until Mint Buttercream and Chocolate Drizzler are set. Cut into squares. Makes 16 to 24.

"Mmm, I love these" is the usual response after one taste.

Minty Brownies

If you love the flavor of Thin Mints, these brownies are destined to make believers out of Girl Scout cookie lovers!

MINTY FILLING
8 oz. cream cheese, softened to room
  temperature
1/4 cup granulated sugar
1 large egg, lightly beaten
1 tsp. pure mint extract (spearmint or
  peppermint)

BROWNIE BASE
4 oz. unsweetened chocolate, coarsely
  chopped
2/3 cup unsalted butter
2 cups granulated sugar
4 large eggs, lightly beaten
1 tsp. pure vanilla extract
1 1/4 cups unbleached, all-purpose flour
1 tsp. baking powder
1 tsp. salt

Heat oven to 350 degrees. Lightly grease and flour a 13x9" baking pan, being sure to tap out any excess flour and discard.

For the Minty Filling: Beat the cream cheese and sugar in a small bowl using an electric mixer until light, fluffy, and smooth. Add egg and mint, mixing well. Set aside.

For the Brownie Base: Melt chocolate and butter in a medium saucepan over low heat, stirring to blend.

Remove saucepan from heat. Whisk in sugar, eggs, and vanilla.

Stir in flour, baking powder, and salt. Spread into prepared pan. Carefully spoon Minty Filling atop Brownie Base. To marble, gently cut through in a zigzag pattern with a knife. Bake for 35 minutes or until a cake tester or toothpick inserted near the center comes out with a few moist crumbs attached. Cool pan completely on a wire rack. Cut into bars. Makes 2 1/2 dozen.

BEV'S BITES ——————
These are delicious "as is," but of course they can be frosted with one of my bitter-sweet chocolate frostings, adding 1/4 tsp. pure mint extract to the frosting and blending well.

My Brownie Base is Plain and Simple Fudgy Brownies (see index) with nuts omitted.

Saucepan Brownies with German Chocolate Topping

The first time I made a German chocolate cake, I completely covered the cake (top and sides) with its traditional coconut and pecan topping. This recipe is my easier way of enjoying these tastes.

BROWNIE BASE

½ cup unsalted butter
2 oz. unsweetened chocolate, coarsely chopped
1 cup granulated sugar
1 tsp. pure vanilla extract
2 large eggs, lightly beaten
⅔ cup unbleached, all-purpose flour
½ tsp. baking powder
¼ tsp. salt

GERMAN CHOCOLATE TOPPING

2 tbsp. unsalted butter, melted
½ cup firmly packed dark brown sugar
2 tbsp. dark corn syrup or brown rice syrup
2 tbsp. milk, whole or 2 percent
1 cup sweetened toasted coconut
½ cup coarsely chopped salted pecans, toasted

BEV'S BITE

My Brownie Base is Saucepan Brownies (see index) with nuts omitted.

Heat oven to 350 degrees. Lightly grease an 8" square pan.

For the Brownie Base: Melt the butter and chocolate in a medium saucepan over low heat, stirring constantly.

Remove saucepan from heat; cool slightly. Whisk in sugar and vanilla. Blend in eggs.

Whisk in flour, baking powder, and salt until blended. Spread into prepared pan. Bake for 20 to 25 minutes or until a cake tester or toothpick inserted in the center comes out with a few moist crumbs attached. Cool pan on a wire rack for 30 minutes. Remove entire Brownie Base from pan.

For the German Chocolate Topping: Combine butter, sugar, syrup, and milk in a small bowl, blending well. Toss in coconut and pecans; blend. Gently spread atop Brownie Base, then using a small blow torch (the kind you see chefs use for crème brûlée or you use for welding!), run a flame quickly back and forth over the topping until mixture is bubbly and turns a golden brown, being careful not to burn the topping or your kitchen!

Let brownies cool *completely* for at least 30 minutes (remember, they're *hot!*—you just "blow torched" 'em!). Cut into bars. Makes 16.

WHITE CHOCOLATE VERSIONS

Baking with chocolate is a little like magic . . . full of delights and surprises, as in these White Chocolate Round Brownies!

Brownie Wedgies with White and Dark Chocolate Chunks

I love to make "brownies in the round"—it gives a whole new, tasteful meaning to wedgies!

BROWNIE BASE
Unsweetened cocoa powder, sifted
5 oz. white chocolate, coarsely chopped, divided
6 tbsp. unsalted butter
¾ cup granulated sugar
1 tsp. pure vanilla extract
2 large eggs, lightly beaten
½ cup unbleached, all-purpose flour
½ tsp. salt
2 oz. semisweet chocolate, coarsely chopped

Heat oven to 350 degrees. Lightly grease an 8" round cake pan. Sprinkle bottom with cocoa powder, tapping out any excess.

For the Brownie Base: Melt 4 oz. of the white chocolate with butter in a small saucepan over low heat. Stir until smooth.

Remove saucepan from heat. Cool mixture for 15 minutes.

Whisk in sugar and vanilla until blended. Whisk in eggs, until glossy and smooth. Stir in flour and salt just until mixture is combined. Gently stir in remaining white chocolate and semisweet chocolate. Spread into prepared pan. Bake for 20 to 30 minutes or until a cake tester or toothpick inserted near the center comes out with a few moist crumbs attached. Cool pan completely on a wire rack. Cut into wedges. Makes 8 to 12.

Macadamia-Nut White Brownies

Most bakeries have a version of this rich brownie, and some are tasty. Use only the best ingredients for my version and do not underbake.

BROWNIE BASE

10 oz. white chocolate, coarsely chopped, divided
6 tbsp. unsalted butter
2 large eggs, lightly beaten
¾ cup granulated sugar
¼ cup firmly packed light brown sugar
½ tsp. pure vanilla extract
1½ cups unbleached, all-purpose flour
½ tsp. baking powder
¼ tsp. salt
¾ cup coarsely chopped macadamia nuts, toasted

BEV'S BITE

These brownies are better the next morning, or evening if you care to wait that long!

Heat oven to 350 degrees. Lightly grease and flour a 9″ square pan, being sure to tap out excess flour.

For the Brownie Base: Melt 7 oz. of the white chocolate and butter in a medium saucepan over low heat, stirring often until mixture is smooth and well blended. Remove saucepan from heat; cool.

In a large bowl of an electric mixer, on medium-high speed beat eggs, sugars, and vanilla until mixture is blended and very smooth and light. Blend in chocolate mixture, beating until smooth.

Add flour, baking powder, and salt to the mixer bowl—a little at a time—stopping often to scrape bowl and paddle. Gently stir in nuts and remaining white chocolate. Spread into prepared pan. Bake for 35 minutes or until a cake tester or toothpick inserted near the center comes out with a few moist crumbs attached. Cool pan completely on a wire rack. Cut into squares. Makes 12 to 16.

Snow-White Raspberry Brownies

Even the Seven Dwarfs wouldn't object to eating these on a regular basis! This is more like a white chocolate bar, but who cares what you call it . . . the flavors are divine. My mom used to make something very similar (once she got on the "brownie bandwagon")—a delicate crust, a filling, a crumb topping, and using semisweet chocolate instead of the white—and I've adapted it and streamlined the process.

BROWNIE BASE

1½ cups unsalted butter, softened to
   room temperature
1 cup granulated sugar
½ cup firmly packed light brown sugar
1 tsp. pure vanilla extract
½ tsp. salt
4 cups unbleached, all-purpose flour
2 large eggs, lighten beaten
2 cups seedless red raspberry preserves
6 oz. white chocolate, coarsely chopped

Heat oven to 350 degrees.

For the Brownie Base: In a large bowl of an electric mixer, beat the butter and sugars on medium until mixture is smooth and creamy. Add vanilla and salt and beat until blended.

Beat in flour, a little at a time. When mixture is crumbly, remove 1 cup from bowl and set aside.

Add eggs to mixing bowl, blending well to form a dough. Press dough into an ungreased 13x9" baking pan, then prick dough lightly all over with a fork. Bake for 25 minutes or until dough is a light golden color. Cool pan on a wire rack for 10 minutes.

In a small bowl, vigorously beat preserves with a wooden spoon by hand (this helps soften them up and make them easier to spread!—and they know you mean business). Carefully spread preserves over partially baked dough. Scatter white chocolate over preserves, and then top with that crumb mixture you set aside.

Bake for an additional 20 minutes or until the topping is light golden and the aromas are driving you mad! Cool pan completely on a wire rack. Cut into bars. Makes 3 dozen.

BEV'S BITE —————————

If fresh raspberries are in season, serve these bars on a dessert plate that has first been sprinkled with confectioners' sugar—then garnish the plate with some fresh red raspberries.

White Chocolate Brownies Studded with Dried Fruits

Lots of dried fruits combine to make these white-chocolate treats sweet and fruity. And that chocolate crumb topping is "oh so good"!

BROWNIE BASE
12 oz. white chocolate, coarsely chopped, divided
½ cup unsalted butter
2 large eggs, lightly beaten
¼ cup granulated sugar
1¼ cups unbleached, all-purpose flour
⅓ cup fresh orange juice
½ tsp. salt
⅓ cup coarsely chopped dried apricots
⅓ cup coarsely chopped dried mangoes
¼ cup coarsely chopped dried cherries
2 tbsp. firmly packed light brown sugar
⅓ cup coarsely chopped toasted pecans

Heat oven to 325 degrees. Lightly grease a 9" square pan.

For the Brownie Base: Melt 6 oz. of the white chocolate and butter in a small saucepan over low heat, stirring until mixture is smooth and blended. Remove saucepan from heat; set aside.

In a large bowl of an electric mixer, beat eggs and sugar on medium-high speed until light and fluffy.

With mixer on low speed, add chocolate mixture, flour, juice, and salt. Mix, stopping to scrape the bowl and paddle, just until combined. Fold in fruits. Spread into prepared pan. Bake for 12 minutes or until the edges are light golden.

While mixture is baking, combine in a medium bowl the remaining white chocolate, brown sugar, and pecans. Remove Brownie Base from oven, sprinkle chocolate/pecan mixture evenly atop, then return to oven and continue baking for an additional 15 minutes until golden brown. Cool pan completely on a wire rack. Cut into squares. Makes 2 dozen.

Hey! Didn't that troll just take a bite of my brownie?!

White Chocolate Chunk Butterscotch Brownies

Recipes for butterscotch versions of brownies abound, but my all-time favorite is one I created for a White Chocolate Sensations cooking class, using what makes homemade taste extra special. In this case, it's the addition of lots and lots of excellent white chocolate chunks (and a few bittersweet for good luck)!

BROWNIE BASE

1 cup unsalted butter, softened to
　room temperature
1 cup firmly packed light brown sugar
½ cup firmly packed dark brown sugar
2 large eggs, lightly beaten
1 tsp. pure vanilla extract
1 cup unbleached, all-purpose flour
1½ tsp. baking powder
½ tsp. salt
5 oz. white chocolate, coarsely chopped
3 oz. bittersweet chocolate, coarsely
　chopped

BEV'S BITES ⎯⎯⎯⎯⎯

This makes a thin brownie that's crusty on top and soft in the center.

Another thing that makes these taste "oh so great": Billington's brown sugars. Check out my ingredients chapter for more information.

Heat oven to 350 degrees. Lightly grease a 13x9" baking pan.

For the Brownie Base: In a large bowl of an electric mixer, beat the butter with sugars on medium speed until light and fluffy, stopping often to scrape bowl and paddle. Add eggs and vanilla and mix.

Add flour, baking powder, and salt a little at a time, at low speed, stopping often to scrape bowl and paddle and mixing just until combined. Stir in chocolates. Spread into prepared pan. Bake for 25 minutes or until top is done and a cake tester or toothpick inserted near the center comes out with a few moist crumbs attached. Cool pan completely on a wire rack. Cut into bars. Makes 2 to 3 dozen.

White Chocolate Round Brownies

And who's to say a brownie can't be round? Not me . . . or you. Just mix, bake, and enjoy whatever shape they're in.

BROWNIE BASE
4 oz. white chocolate, coarsely chopped
1 cup unsalted butter, softened to room temperature, divided
¾ cup granulated sugar
¼ cup firmly packed light brown sugar
2 large eggs, lightly beaten
1½ tsp. pure vanilla extract
2 cups unbleached, all-purpose flour
½ cup unsweetened cocoa powder, sifted
1 tsp. baking soda
¼ tsp. salt
8 oz. semisweet chocolate chips

BEV'S BITE ——————
Try this delicious, easy-to-make treat as an accompaniment to crème brûlée!

Heat oven to 325 degrees. Line 2 or 3 cookie sheets with parchment paper.

For the Brownie Base: Melt the white chocolate and ¼ cup butter in a small saucepan over low heat, stirring until mixture is blended and smooth. Remove saucepan from heat; allow to cool.

In a large bowl of an electric mixer, blend remaining butter with sugars on medium-high speed until mixture is light and fluffy. Beat in eggs, stopping occasionally and scraping bowl and paddle. Add white-chocolate mixture and vanilla and beat on medium speed until combined.

Add flour, cocoa powder, baking soda, and salt a little at a time, mixing at low speed and stopping often to scrape bowl and paddle. Mix in just until combined—do not overbeat. Stir in semisweet chips.

Drop dough with a tablespoon-size "disher" or tablespoon measure on the cookie sheets. (Cookies will spread as they bake. Don't scoop too close together!) Bake for 15 to 20 minutes or until the edges are just beginning to turn a light golden brown.

Cool for a few minutes on cookie sheets, then remove individual cookies to a wire rack and allow to cool completely. (Yeah, right!) Makes about 2½ dozen.

DERIVATIONS ON A THEME

Is it a pie? Or cake? Or—who cares? Walnut Fudge Brownie with
Ganache and Caramel Sauce has sensual flavors with a gooey sauce.

Bev's Superchocolaty Cookies

I obviously feel that there are endless possibilities when I combine chocolate and cookies and have brownies on my mind!

BROWNIE BASE
6 oz. semisweet chocolate, coarsely
    chopped
2 oz. unsweetened chocolate, coarsely
    chopped
6 tbsp. unsalted butter, softened to
    room temperature
2 large eggs, lightly beaten
1 tbsp. unsweetened cocoa powder,
    sifted
2 tsp. pure vanilla extract
$^3/_4$ cup granulated sugar
$^1/_3$ cup unbleached, all-purpose flour
1 tsp. baking powder
$^1/_2$ tsp. salt
$^1/_2$ cup finely ground walnuts
$1^1/_2$ cups coarsely chopped walnuts,
    toasted
6 oz. milk chocolate chips

Heat oven to 325 degrees. Line 3 cookie sheets with parchment paper.

For the Brownie Base: Melt the semisweet and unsweetened chocolates and butter in a medium saucepan over low heat, stirring until mixture is blended and smooth. Remove saucepan from heat; set aside.

In a large bowl of an electric mixer, beat eggs, cocoa powder, and vanilla on medium speed until blended. Blend in sugar until mixture is well blended and creamy. Beat in chocolate mixture on medium-low speed until combined.

Stir in flour, baking powder, salt, and ground nuts, stopping occasionally to scrape bowl and paddle. Gently fold in nut pieces and chocolate chips. Scoop batter with a $^1/_3$ cup dry measuring cup and drop onto prepared sheets. (Batter will spread during baking; don't scoop too close together!) Bake for 12 minutes. These cookies are deceiving: when they're done, they're still soft and wet looking inside, but they will firm up as they cool. It's sad but true—if you overbake them you'll know it, because they'll be dry.

Cool sheets completely on a wire rack. Makes about 1 dozen.

Chocolate Chocolate Cocoa Cookies

Here is another variation on the cookie/brownie theme, this one with an intense cocoa and chocolate flavor.

BROWNIE BASE

4 oz. unsweetened chocolate, coarsely chopped

6 oz. semisweet chocolate, coarsely chopped

½ cup unsalted butter, softened to room temperature

4 large eggs, lightly beaten

1 cup granulated sugar

½ cup firmly packed light brown sugar

1½ tbsp. unsweetened cocoa powder, sifted

2 tsp. pure vanilla extract

½ cup unbleached, all-purpose flour

¼ tsp. salt

½ tsp. baking powder

2 oz. bittersweet chocolate, coarsely chopped

Heat oven to 350 degrees. Line 2 or 3 cookie sheets with parchment paper.

For the Brownie Base: Combine the unsweetened and semisweet chocolates in a double boiler set over simmering water. Stir often, over low heat, until mixture is melted and smooth.

Remove top of double boiler from heat, and carefully wipe bottom (so none of the moisture steams up into the chocolate mixture). Whisk in butter to blend, then set aside.

In a large bowl of an electric mixer, beat eggs and sugars on medium-high speed until mixture is thick and well blended. Beat in cocoa and vanilla, stopping occasionally to scrape sides of bowl and paddle. Stir in flour, salt, and baking powder.

On low speed, gently blend in chocolate mixture. Stir in chocolate pieces. Cover batter and chill for puffiest cookies (at least 1 hour or up to 24).

Drop by heaping tablespoonfuls onto prepared cookie sheets. (Batter will spread during baking; don't scoop too close together!) Bake for 9 to 10 minutes until cookies are puffy. Cool sheets completely on a wire rack. Makes 2½ to 3 dozen.

Fudgy Brownie Cookies

These delicious alternatives to a square brownie contain three types of chocolate. Excellent!

BROWNIE BASE
3 oz. semisweet chocolate, coarsely chopped
3 oz. bittersweet chocolate, coarsely chopped
⅓ cup unsalted butter, softened to room temperature
¾ cup granulated sugar
2 large eggs, lightly beaten
½ cup unbleached, all-purpose flour
¼ tsp. baking powder
⅛ tsp. salt
4 oz. milk chocolate, coarsely chopped
½ cup finely chopped pecans, toasted

Heat oven to 350 degrees. Line 3 cookie sheets with parchment paper.

For the Brownie Base: Combine the semisweet and bittersweet chocolates in a double boiler set over simmering water. Stir often, over low heat, until mixture is melted and smooth.

Remove top of double boiler from heat, and carefully wipe bottom (so none of the moisture steams up into the chocolate mixture). Whisk in butter, then set aside to cool.

In a large bowl of an electric mixer, beat sugar and eggs until well blended. Gradually blend in chocolate mixture. Add flour, baking powder, and salt a little at a time, stopping often to scrape bowl and paddle. Mix on medium speed until well blended. Gently add in chocolate pieces and nuts.

Drop by spoonfuls or with a cookie scoop (disher) on prepared cookie sheets. (Batter will spread during baking; don't scoop too close together!) Bake for 8 to 12 minutes or until cookie tops spring back when gently touched. For the best-tasting cookies, do not overbake. Cool sheets completely on a wire rack. Makes about 3 dozen.

Nearly Flourless Divine Brownie Cookies

This recipe is based on my eating adventures. I've tasted (and adored) something similar served to me with a tall glass of cold milk in a Montreal restaurant. If I'd known the dessert was going to be that good, I would have skipped the meal!

BROWNIE BASE

4 oz. bittersweet chocolate, coarsely chopped

7 oz. semisweet chocolate, coarsely chopped, divided

2 oz. milk chocolate, coarsely chopped

2 tbsp. unsalted butter, softened to room temperature

½ cup granulated sugar

2 large eggs, room temperature

1 tsp. pure vanilla extract

¼ cup unbleached, all-purpose flour

¼ tsp. baking powder

⅛ tsp. salt

1½ cups coarsely chopped, toasted salted pecans

Heat oven to 350 degrees. Line 2 or 3 cookie sheets with parchment paper.

For the Brownie Base: Combine the bittersweet, 2 oz. semisweet, and all the milk chocolate in a double boiler set over simmering water. Stir often, over low heat, until mixture is melted and smooth.

In a large bowl of an electric mixer, beat butter and sugar at medium speed until light and fluffy. Add eggs and vanilla, beating to blend. On low speed, stir in flour, baking powder, and salt, stopping occasionally to scrape bowl and paddle.

Add chocolate mixture, stirring just until combined. Add nuts and remaining chocolate pieces. Scoop batter by rounded tablespoonfuls and drop onto prepared sheets. (Batter will spread during baking; don't scoop too close together!) Bake for 12 minutes or until tops look dry (cookies will still be slightly moist but will firm up when cool). Overbaking these is against the law in many states! Cool sheets completely on a wire rack. Pour yourself a tall cold one (milk, that is!) and do a taste test. Makes about 2 dozen.

Refrigerator Brownie Cookies

The first time someone told me they were making refrigerator cookies, I thought that meant they didn't need to be baked—that they were "cooking" in the fridge! Fortunately, I've learned the truth. This recipe is an adaptation of one my husband's mom, Jane, always made.

BROWNIE BASE

3 oz. semisweet chocolate, coarsely
    chopped
3 oz. milk chocolate, coarsely chopped
1 cup granulated sugar
½ cup firmly packed light brown sugar
1 cup unsalted butter, softened to
    room temperature
1 large egg, lightly beaten
1½ tsp. pure vanilla extract
2½ cups unbleached, all-purpose flour
1½ tsp. baking powder
¼ tsp. salt
2 oz. bittersweet chocolate, coarsely
    chopped
½ cup finely chopped walnuts, toasted

For the Brownie Base: Combine the semisweet and milk chocolates in a double boiler set over simmering water. Stir often, over low heat, until mixture is melted and smooth.

Remove top of double boiler from heat, and carefully wipe bottom (so none of the moisture steams up into the chocolate mixture); set aside to cool slightly.

In a large bowl of an electric mixer, beat sugars and butter on medium speed, stopping and scraping bowl and paddle often, until light and fluffy. Add melted chocolate and combine. On low speed, stir in egg and vanilla.

Stir in flour, baking powder, and salt until blended. Add chocolate pieces and nuts.

Divide dough in half and shape into two 10 to 12"-long logs. Wrap each log in plastic wrap and refrigerate until firm. (This takes about 2 hours.)

Heat oven to 350 degrees. Cut rolls into ½"-thick slices with a sharp serrated knife. Place 1" apart on ungreased cookie sheets. Bake for 12 to 14 minutes or until cookies are set. Cool sheets completely on a wire rack. Makes about 4 dozen.

Scoop and Drop Brownies in the Round

These are just delicious—crusty on the outside, soft on the inside. Very little flour makes for a very intense chocolate flavor, especially if you enjoy these while they're still warm. I created these for a Gifts from the Kitchen cooking class, and they're always a hit with the bakers (gift givers) and receivers!

BROWNIE BASE

6 oz. semisweet chocolate, coarsely chopped
6 oz. bittersweet chocolate, coarsely chopped, divided
3½ tbsp. unsalted butter, softened to room temperature
¾ cup granulated sugar
½ tsp. pure vanilla extract
2 large eggs, lightly beaten
¼ cup unbleached, all-purpose flour
¼ tsp. baking powder
⅛ tsp. salt
2 cups coarsely chopped walnuts, toasted

Heat oven to 325 degrees. Line 3 cookie sheets with parchment paper.

For the Brownie Base: Combine the semisweet chocolate and 3½ oz. bittersweet chocolate in a double boiler set over simmering water. Stir often, over low heat, until mixture is melted and smooth.

Remove top of double boiler from heat, and carefully wipe bottom (so none of the moisture steams up into the chocolate mixture); set aside to cool slightly.

In a large bowl of an electric mixer, beat butter, sugar, and vanilla on medium-high speed until light and fluffy, stopping occasionally to scrape sides of bowl and paddle. Add eggs, beating to combine.

Add chocolate mixture on low speed. Gently add in flour, baking powder, and salt, stopping occasionally to scrape sides of bowl and paddle. Add remaining chocolate pieces and nuts. Stir to combine. Drop by heaping tablespoonfuls onto prepared sheets. (Batter will spread during baking; don't scoop too close together!) Bake for 12 to 15 minutes (no longer—for ultimate crisp tops and cake-like texture inside, don't overbake). Cool sheets completely on a wire rack. Makes about 18.

Truffle Brownie Cookies

Created for food articles I've written on holiday cookies, this is a take on our favorite Mexican wedding cookie—with a rich chocolate taste. Is this a brownie or a cookie or a chocolate truffle? It's all three of these decadent tastes rolled into one. Call it whatever you'd like—just mix, bake, and enjoy!

BROWNIE BASE
6 oz. bittersweet chocolate, coarsely
  chopped, divided
1 cup unsalted butter, softened to
  room temperature
½ cup + 3 tbsp. confectioners' sugar,
  sifted, divided
1 tsp. pure vanilla extract
1 tsp. pure chocolate extract
2 cups unbleached, all-purpose flour
¼ cup + 4 tbsp. unsweetened cocoa
  powder, sifted, divided
¼ tsp. salt

Heat oven to 375 degrees. Line 2 or 3 cookie sheets with parchment paper.

For the Brownie Base: Place 1 oz. bittersweet chocolate in a double boiler set over simmering water. Stir often, over low heat, until chocolate is melted and smooth.

Remove top of double boiler from heat, and carefully wipe bottom (so none of the moisture steams up into the chocolate). Set aside to cool slightly.

In a large bowl of an electric mixer, beat butter and ½ cup sugar until light and fluffy, stopping occasionally to scrape bowl and paddle. Add extracts and melted chocolate; blend on low speed until combined. Stir in flour, ¼ cup cocoa powder, and salt. Blend in remaining bittersweet pieces. Scoop into balls (use heaping teaspoon measure to make them about ¾" in size) and place on prepared sheets. Bake for 10 minutes or until just firm to the touch. Cool sheets completely on a wire rack.

Combine remaining sugar and cocoa powder in a shallow pan. Whisk until well blended. Roll cooled cookies in mixture. Makes about 3 dozen.

Chocolate-Chunk Blondie Cookies

Kahlua gives these chunky, chocolaty cookies that extra-special something!

BLONDIE BASE

1 cup unsalted butter, softened to
    room temperature
½ cup firmly packed light brown sugar
¾ cup granulated sugar
2 tbsp. pure vanilla extract
2 tbsp. Kahlua
2 large eggs, lightly beaten
2½ cups unbleached, all-purpose flour
1 tsp. baking soda
½ tsp. salt
1 cup coarsely chopped almonds, toasted
5 oz. bittersweet chocolate, coarsely
    chopped

Heat oven to 350 degrees. Line 2 or 3 cookie sheets with parchment paper.

For the Blondie Base: In a large bowl with an electric mixer, beat the butter with sugars at medium speed, stopping and scraping the bowl often, until light and fluffy. Blend in vanilla, Kahlua, and eggs.

On low speed, stir in flour, baking soda, and salt. Mix in nuts and chocolate.

Scoop dough by rounded tablespoonfuls onto prepared sheets. (Batter will spread during baking; don't scoop too close together!) Bake for 12 minutes or until tops spring back when lightly touched and edges are golden. Cool sheets completely on a wire rack. Makes 2 to 3 dozen.

Toffee Brownie Rounds

My husband, John, loves chocolate-covered toffee almost as much as he loves me. These next two recipes were developed to lure him into a trance. (The cookies and bars he loves—the whole trance idea I'm going to have to keep working on!)

BROWNIE BASE
1¼ cups unsalted butter, softened to room temperature
⅔ cup granulated sugar
1 cup firmly packed light brown sugar
2 tbsp. brown rice syrup or light corn syrup
2 large eggs, lightly beaten
2 tsp. pure vanilla extract
3 cups unbleached, all-purpose flour
1 tbsp. baking powder
1½ tsp. salt
8 oz. bittersweet chocolate, coarsely chopped
1½ cups coarsely chopped chocolate toffee candy

Heat oven to 375 degrees. Line 3 cookie sheets with parchment paper.

For the Brownie Base: In a large bowl with an electric mixer, beat the butter and sugars at medium-high speed until light and fluffy. Add syrup, eggs, and vanilla, beating to blend.

Stir in flour, baking powder, and salt, stopping occasionally to scrape bowl and paddle. Gently add chocolate and toffee until combined.

Drop by tablespoonfuls onto prepared sheets. Bake for 12 minutes or until tops spring back when lightly touched. Cool sheets completely on a wire rack. Makes about 2½ dozen.

Toffee Fudgy Bars

This recipe mixes three types of chocolate and, as if that weren't enough, chocolate toffee candy!

BROWNIE BASE
6 oz. unsweetened chocolate, coarsely chopped
4 oz. bittersweet chocolate, coarsely chopped
2 cups coarsely chopped chocolate toffee candy
1½ cups unbleached, all-purpose flour, divided
1 cup unsalted butter, softened to room temperature
2 cups granulated sugar
⅓ cup firmly packed light brown sugar
5 large eggs, lightly beaten
2½ tsp. pure vanilla extract
3 tbsp. unsweetened cocoa powder, sifted
½ tsp. salt
¼ tsp. baking powder

Heat oven to 350 degrees. Lightly grease a 13x9" baking pan.

For the Brownie Base: Combine the chocolates in a double boiler set over simmering water. Stir often, over low heat, until mixture is melted and smooth.

Remove top of double boiler from heat, and carefully wipe bottom (so none of the moisture steams up into the chocolate mixture). Transfer chocolate mixture to a medium bowl.

In a small bowl, toss toffee with 3 tbsp. flour. Set aside.

In a medium bowl with an electric mixer, beat together butter and sugars until light and fluffy. Add chocolate mixture to blend. Add eggs and vanilla, mixing on low speed until combined.

Gently stir in remaining flour, cocoa powder, salt, and baking powder. Stir in toffee. Spread into prepared pan. Bake for 30 minutes or until a cake tester or toothpick comes out with a few moist crumbs attached, testing 1" from the edge of the pan. Cool pan completely on a wire rack. Refrigerate, covered, overnight so flavors can blend well. Cut into bars. Serve with toffee swirl ice cream, if desired. Makes about 2 dozen.

Bring the forks and plates. Whipped cream this soft and a brownie dessert this decadent beg to be eaten quickly.

Brownie Cake Poked with Red Raspberries

An easy Brownie Base is the star of the show in this simple but spectacular cake crowned with raspberries (and some are even poked inside).

BROWNIE BASE

3 oz. unsweetened chocolate, coarsely chopped

½ cup unsalted butter, softened to room temperature

1⅓ cups granulated sugar

2 large eggs, lightly beaten

1 tsp. pure vanilla extract

⅔ cup unbleached, all-purpose flour

3 cups red raspberries, rinsed and lightly dried, divided

1 cup heavy (whipping) cream, whipped

Heat oven to 350 degrees. Lightly grease and flour a 9" springform pan.

For the Brownie Base: Melt the chocolate in a double boiler set over simmering water. Stir often, over low heat, until chocolate is melted and smooth.

Remove top of double boiler from heat, and carefully wipe bottom (so none of the moisture steams up into the chocolate). Whisk in butter to blend.

Whisk in sugar, eggs, and vanilla. Whisk in flour, blending well. Spread into prepared pan. Gently press 1¼ cups raspberries into Brownie Base (surely this means you're poking fun at the Brownie Base?!). Bake for 35 to 40 minutes or until the edges crack and feel firm to the touch. Cool pan completely on a wire rack.

Gently remove sides of springform pan. Cut Brownie Base into wedges. Serve each wedge with a dollop of whipped cream and a sprinkling of remaining red raspberries atop cream. Makes about 8 wedges.

Brownie Banana Split

Secretly, we all wish for a cake base while we're eating that banana split, and a brownie base seems to me to be the perfect solution to this dilemma!

BROWNIE BASE
4 oz. unsweetened chocolate, coarsely chopped
⅔ cup unsalted butter
2 cups granulated sugar
4 large eggs, lightly beaten
1 tsp. pure vanilla extract
1¼ cups unbleached, all-purpose flour
1 tsp. baking powder
1 tsp. salt

BANANA SPLIT TOPPINGS
4 ripe bananas, peeled and thinly sliced
1 qt. vanilla ice cream, softened slightly
1 qt. chocolate ice cream, softened slightly
Sauces of your choice, such as Smooth and Silky Fudge Sauce and In a Hurry Caramel Sauce (see index)
Whipped cream
Fresh seasonal berries, such as strawberries, red raspberries, or blueberries
Chopped toasted peanuts, walnuts, or pecans, if desired

Heat oven to 350 degrees. Lightly grease a 13x9" baking pan.

For the Brownie Base: Melt the chocolate and butter in a medium saucepan over low heat, stirring to blend.

Remove saucepan from heat. Whisk in sugar, eggs, and vanilla.

Stir in flour, baking powder, and salt. Spread into prepared pan. Bake for 25 minutes or until the brownies *just* begin to pull away from the sides of the pan. Brownies will be dry if overbaked! Cool slightly (or just until they will no longer burn the roof of your mouth!). Cut into squares. Place 1 square in an individual dessert dish or banana-split bowl.

For the Banana Split Toppings: Top each brownie with some banana slices and a scoop of vanilla and chocolate ice creams. Drizzle sauces over top, then garnish with whipped cream, berries, and nuts. Makes 2 to 3 dozen.

BEV'S BITES
Want to get your kids involved in baking? This is a great recipe to get them started. And remember, measuring and fractions help their math and science skills, too! (You didn't think you'd use those skills later in life, did you?!)

My Brownie Base is Plain and Simple Fudgy Brownies (see index) with nuts omitted.

Brownie Pudding Layer Cake

Chocolate pudding and sliced strawberries between brownie cake . . . what could be simpler and more satisfying? (I know—two slices!) I'd hate to have you go through all the trouble of using great ingredients and then make 3 cups of instant pudding, so I'm including my favorite chocolate pudding recipe (in case you're feeling ambitious or nostalgic!).

BROWNIE BASE
1 cup unsalted butter
4 oz. unsweetened chocolate, coarsely chopped
2 cups granulated sugar
2 tsp. pure vanilla extract
4 large eggs, lightly beaten
1⅓ cups unbleached, all-purpose flour
1 tsp. baking powder
½ tsp. salt

BEV'S CHOCOLATE PUDDING
½ cup granulated sugar
2 tbsp. cornstarch or arrowroot
⅓ cup unsweetened cocoa powder, sifted
⅛ tsp. salt
2 cups milk, whole or 2 percent
2 large egg yolks, lightly beaten
2 tbsp. unsalted butter, softened to room temperature
2½ tsp. pure vanilla extract

FILLING/TOPPING
4 to 5 cups thinly sliced fresh strawberries (2 pt.)
Confectioners' sugar, sifted

BEV'S BITES
Plastic wrap keeps a "film" from forming on top of the pudding.

My Brownie Base is Saucepan Brownies (see index), doubled and with nuts omitted.

Leftovers? Store in the refrigerator.

Heat oven to 350 degrees. Line two 8" round cake pans with foil; lightly grease foil.

For the Brownie Base: Melt the butter and chocolate in a medium saucepan over low heat, stirring constantly. Remove saucepan from heat; cool slightly.

With a large spoon, blend in sugar and vanilla. Blend in eggs. Stir in flour, baking powder, and salt until blended. Spread into prepared pans. Bake for 20 minutes or until set in the center. Cool pans completely on a wire rack. Remove foil, then freeze for 1 hour or until cakes are firm.

For Bev's Chocolate Pudding: Blend sugar, cornstarch, cocoa powder, and salt in a 2-qt. saucepan.

In a separate bowl, combine milk and egg yolks. Stir into sugar mixture. Cook over medium heat, stirring constantly, until mixture thickens and boils. Boil and stir 1 minute.

Remove saucepan from heat. Stir in butter and vanilla until smooth. Transfer to a mixing bowl, cool for 5 minutes, then immediately press plastic wrap directly on top of pudding, covering. Chill. Makes about 3 cups.

Place one brownie cake on a serving plate. Top with half of the pudding.

For the Filling and Topping: Top the pudding with half of the berries. Place remaining brownie cake atop the berries. Top with remaining pudding and berries. Slice cake and dust each serving with sugar. Makes about 10.

Brownie Coconut Pudding Cake

A pudding cake is an old-fashioned dessert worth revisiting. This recipe is easy to make—soft and chocolaty with a warm pudding that makes itself while the cake bakes. I've updated the version that my aunt, Em, served me whenever I visited her in Newark, New Jersey.

BROWNIE BASE
4 tbsp. unsalted butter, softened to room temperature
¼ cup granulated sugar
½ cup firmly packed light brown sugar
1 cup unbleached, all-purpose flour
⅓ cup unsweetened cocoa powder, sifted
¼ tsp. baking soda
1 tbsp. baking powder
½ tsp. salt
½ cup half-and-half
1 tsp. pure vanilla extract
¾ cup sweetened coconut flakes
½ cup Smooth and Silky Fudge Sauce (see index)
1 cup milk, whole or 2 percent

Heat oven to 350 degrees. Lightly grease an 8" square pan.

For the Brownie Base: In a medium bowl with an electric mixer, beat the butter and sugars until light and fluffy. Add flour, cocoa, baking soda, baking powder, and salt, mixing. Stir in half-and-half and vanilla. Add coconut, stirring to blend. Spread into prepared pan.

In a small saucepan, heat and whisk together sauce and milk until hot and smooth. Carefully pour evenly over Brownie Base. Bake for 35 minutes or until top is crusty. Serve warm, with a small scoop of vanilla ice cream or some whipped cream, if desired. Makes 6 to 8 servings.

"I Can Frost Myself, Thank You" Brownie Cake

This recipe takes the cake when you want something quick, easy, and homemade.

BROWNIE BASE
½ cup unsalted butter
1⅓ cup granulated sugar
½ cup unsweetened cocoa powder, sifted
2 large eggs, lightly beaten
1 tsp. pure vanilla extract
1½ cups unbleached, all-purpose flour
⅔ cups milk, whole or 2 percent
1 tsp. baking powder
½ tsp. baking soda
½ tsp. salt

FROSTING, THANK YOU
¾ cup firmly packed light brown sugar
10 oz. semisweet chocolate, finely chopped

Heat oven to 350 degrees. Lightly grease a 13x9" baking pan.

For the Brownie Base: Melt the butter in a medium saucepan.

Remove saucepan from heat. Whisk in sugar and cocoa powder to blend.

Add eggs and vanilla. Mix *just* until combined. Whisk in flour, milk, baking powder, baking soda, and salt, beating until well combined. Spread into prepared pan.

For the Frosting, Thank You: In a small bowl, gently stir the ingredients to combine. Sprinkle atop Brownie Base in pan. Bake for 30 minutes or until a cake tester or toothpick inserted near the center comes out with a few moist crumbs attached. Cool pan completely on a wire rack. Cut into bars. Makes 12 to 18.

Brownie Maple Cupcakes with Chocolate Maple Fluff Frosting

Cupcakes are everyone's favorite treat—young and old alike—and they often get overlooked in our haste to make something quick and easy. Slow down a few seconds and bake these tempting brownies in cupcake form. And top them with this maple frosting. Yum!

Heat oven to 350 degrees. Line 16 muffin cups with cupcake liners.

For the Brownie Base: Melt the chocolate and butter in a medium saucepan over low heat, stirring to blend.

Remove saucepan from heat. Whisk in sugar, eggs, and maple.

Stir in flour, baking powder, salt, and nuts. Spoon about ⅓ cup batter into each cupcake liner. Bake for 25 minutes or until set. Cool completely on a wire rack.

For the Chocolate Maple Fluff Frosting: Combine chocolate and cream in a double boiler set over simmering water. Stir often, over low heat, until mixture is melted and smooth.

Remove top of double boiler from heat, and carefully wipe bottom (so none of the moisture steams up into the chocolate mixture). Transfer chocolate mixture to a medium bowl. Set aside to cool for 30 minutes. Refrigerate to chill thoroughly.

In a large bowl of an electric mixer, beat sugar, butter, and maple until well blended. Gradually add chilled chocolate mixture and, with the whisk attachment, beat until mixture is stiff. Spread or pipe with pastry bag atop cupcakes. Makes 16.

BROWNIE BASE
4 oz. unsweetened chocolate, coarsely chopped
⅔ cup unsalted butter
2 cups granulated sugar
4 large eggs, lightly beaten
1 tsp. pure maple extract
1¼ cups unbleached, all-purpose flour
1 tsp. baking powder
1 tsp. salt
1 cup chopped walnuts or pecans, lightly toasted

CHOCOLATE MAPLE FLUFF FROSTING
3 oz. bittersweet chocolate, finely chopped
½ cup heavy (whipping) cream
1½ cups confectioners' sugar, sifted
½ cup unsalted butter, softened to room temperature
½ tsp. pure maple extract

BEV'S BITE ——————
My Brownie Base is Plain and Simple Fudgy Brownies and my Frosting is Chocolate Whipped Cream Frosting (see index), each with an omission and addition.

Peanut Butter Brownie Muffins Topped with Fudge Swirl Ice Cream

Chocolate and peanut butter is such a delightful combination. It brings out the kid in all of us (the good kid, that is!).

BROWNIE BASE

4 oz. unsweetened chocolate, coarsely
    chopped
²⁄₃ cup unsalted butter
2 cups granulated sugar
4 large eggs, lightly beaten
1 tsp. pure vanilla extract
1¼ cups unbleached, all-purpose flour
1 tsp. baking powder
1 tsp. salt
1 cup chopped peanuts, lightly toasted

MUFFIN STUFF

20 mini chocolate peanut butter cups
1 qt. fudge swirl ice cream

BEV'S BITES

I'm sure you've noticed after assembling your muffins that you now have 2 chocolate peanut butter cups left over. What are you waiting for? Unwrap and enjoy them while the muffins are baking!

My Brownie Base is Plain and Simple Fudgy Brownies (see index) substituting peanuts for other nuts in the recipe.

Heat oven to 350 degrees. Lightly grease 1½ dozen muffin cups.

For the Brownie Base: Melt the chocolate and butter in a medium saucepan over low heat, stirring to blend.

Remove saucepan from heat. Whisk in sugar, eggs, and vanilla.

Stir in flour, baking powder, salt, and nuts. Spoon into muffin cups (filling each cup ¾ full).

For the Muffin Stuff: Top each muffin batter cup with 1 peanut butter cup. Bake for 25 minutes or until a cake tester or toothpick inserted at the edge comes out with a few moist crumbs attached. Cool completely on a wire rack. Then scoop ice cream atop each muffin. Makes 1½ dozen.

Brownie Parfaits

Take any Brownie Base from my "Classic Brownies" chapter, layer, and enjoy.

BROWNIE BASE OPTIONS
Crusty-Top, Soft-Center Brownies
Saucepan Brownies

LAYERS
½ gal. vanilla ice cream
Sauces of your choice, such as In a
    Hurry Caramel Sauce or Smooth and
    Silky Fudge Sauce (see index)
Whipped cream

OPTIONAL LAYERS
Fresh seasonal berries, such as
    strawberries or red raspberries
Toasted salted peanuts or pecans,
    coarsely chopped

For the Brownie Base: Bake and cool your choice of Brownie Base. Cut into small squares (about 1").

For the Layers: In dessert dishes, layer brownies with ice cream and drizzles of caramel or fudge sauce (or both!). Top with whipped cream and optional berries and nuts. Makes 8 to 12!

For my entrée, I'll have grilled wild salmon and a glass of water. I'm saving room for a Brownie Parfait!

One taste, and you'll never be satisfied with plain ol'
strawberry shortcake again.

Brownie Shortcakes

A brownie version of berry shortcake . . . wow! I developed this recipe for a Celebration of Seasonal Fruits cooking class.

BROWNIE BASE
½ cup + 3 tbsp. heavy (whipping) cream, divided
¼ cup + 1 tbsp. Smooth and Silky Fudge Sauce (see index)
1 tsp. pure vanilla extract
1½ cups unbleached, all-purpose flour
½ cup granulated sugar
⅓ cup unsweetened cocoa powder, sifted
1 tbsp. baking powder
½ tsp. salt
¼ cup *cold* unsalted butter, cut into pieces

FILLINGS/TOPPING
Vanilla or fudge swirl ice cream
Fresh seasonal berries, such as strawberries, red raspberries, and blueberries
Smooth and Silky Fudge Sauce

BEV'S BITE ———————
No food processor? Use an electric mixer.

Heat oven to 400 degrees. Line 1 or 2 cookie sheets with parchment paper.

For the Brownie Base: In a small bowl, whisk together ½ cup + 1 tbsp. cream, sauce, and vanilla until smooth.

In a food processor fitted with the metal blade, combine flour, sugar, cocoa powder, baking powder, and salt, pulsing until blended. Add cold butter pieces, pulsing until mixture resembles coarse crumbs. Quickly add cream mixture, pulsing just until a moist dough forms.

Remove dough to a lightly floured work surface. Gently pat dough into a 2"-high disc. Using a 1½ to 2" round biscuit cutter, cut 6 equal pieces, patting and shaping dough as needed to use it all. Place 2½"apart on cookie sheet(s). Brush tops of each round with remaining cream. Bake for 15 minutes or until a cake tester or toothpick inserted in the center comes out with a few moist crumbs attached. Cool sheet(s) completely on wire a rack.

For the Fillings: Cut rounds in half horizontally. Place bottoms on serving plates, and top with ice cream and berries. Add shortcake tops.

For the Topping: Drizzle sauce over shortcakes. Makes 6.

Ice Cream Brownie Pie

Brownie pie is so much fun to order out that I created my own version for "ordering in"!

BROWNIE BASE

¼ cup unsalted butter
1 oz. unsweetened chocolate, coarsely chopped
½ cup granulated sugar
½ tsp. pure vanilla extract
1 large egg, lightly beaten
⅓ cup unbleached, all-purpose flour
¼ tsp. baking powder
¼ tsp. salt

TOPPINGS

¾ cup **In a Hurry Caramel Sauce** (see index)
1 qt. fudge swirl ice cream, slightly softened
¾ cup **Smooth and Silky Fudge Sauce** (see index)
2 tbsp. finely grated bittersweet chocolate
2 tbsp. finely grated white chocolate

Heat oven to 350 degrees. Lightly grease a 9" pie pan.

For the Brownie Base: Melt the butter and chocolate in a medium saucepan over low heat, stirring constantly. Remove saucepan from heat; cool slightly.

Whisk in sugar and vanilla. Blend in egg.

Whisk in flour, baking powder, and salt until blended. Spread into prepared pan. Bake for 15 to 20 minutes or until top of Brownie Base springs back when lightly touched in the center. Cool pan completely on a wire rack.

For the Toppings: Spread caramel sauce over cooled Brownie Base. Top with ice cream, spreading to edges. Drizzle with fudge sauce and set in freezer for 1 hour.

Remove from freezer and quickly cover with plastic wrap. Return to freezer and freeze until firm. Cut into wedges while still frozen. Garnish each wedge with a bit of the grated chocolates. Makes 8 to 12.

Smooth-as-Fudge Brownie Pie

My mom was a great pie baker, and this luscious brownie in a flaky crust was one of my favorite comfort foods when I was a kid (once she got on the "brownie bandwagon"). I include here my favorite pie-dough recipe for the crust.

BROWNIE CRUST
1½ cups unbleached, all-purpose flour
½ tsp. salt
¼ tsp. granulated sugar
5½ tbsp. *cold* unsalted butter, cut into pieces
3 tbsp. cold vegetable shortening
¼ cup ice water

FILLING
¼ cup unsalted butter, softened to room temperature
¼ cup granulated sugar
¼ cup firmly packed light brown sugar
3 large eggs, lightly beaten
½ tsp. pure vanilla extract
½ cup light corn syrup or brown rice syrup
⅓ cup unsweetened cocoa powder, sifted
1 tbsp. unbleached, all-purpose flour

MOM'S WHIPPED TOPPING
1 cup heavy (whipping) cream
2 tbsp. confectioners' sugar, sifted
1 tsp. pure vanilla powder
¼ cup unsweetened cocoa powder

Heat oven to 375 degrees.

For the Brownie Crust: Combine the flour, salt, and sugar in the work bowl of a food processor; pulse until mixed. Add cold butter and shortening, pulsing until mixture forms a coarse meal. Add ice water, a little at a time, just until mixture comes together.

Gently gather into a ball, then flatten and shape into a disc; cover with plastic wrap and refrigerate at least 1 hour (ideally overnight if you can plan ahead). This makes enough for a 2-crust 9" pie or 2 single-crust pies.

When ready to roll out dough, cut disc in half and soften slightly at room temperature. Roll atop a lightly floured surface. Fit into 9" pie pan, fluting or shaping edges as your talents allow.

For the Brownie Filling: In a medium bowl with an electric mixer, beat butter and sugars on medium-high speed until light and fluffy. Blend in eggs, vanilla, syrup, cocoa, and flour, beating on medium-low speed until well combined. Gently spread into prepared crust. Bake for 35 to 40 minutes or until a cake tester or toothpick inserted in the center comes out clean. Cool pan completely on a wire rack.

For Mom's Whipped Topping: In a small bowl with an electric mixer, beat cream until stiff peaks form. Fold in sugar and vanilla. Spoon Topping over cooled pie (or decoratively pipe over pie). Refrigerate for 30 minutes, then slice and sift cocoa over each slice. Makes about 8 slices.

Brownie Wedgies with Caramel Sauce

I love to make this for dinner guests because it's relatively easy and looks (and tastes) divine. Having one of the caramel sauces on hand in the refrigerator makes for a quick and easy drizzle.

BROWNIE BASE
½ cup unsalted butter
2 oz. unsweetened chocolate, coarsely chopped
1 cup granulated sugar
1 tsp. pure vanilla extract
2 large eggs, lightly beaten
⅔ cup unbleached, all-purpose flour
½ tsp. baking powder
¼ tsp. salt

TOPPING
1 tbsp. heavy (whipping) cream or half-and-half
1 cup In a Hurry Caramel Sauce or All the Time in the World Caramel Sauce (see index)
1 oz. white chocolate, coarsely chopped

BEV'S BITE ——————
My Brownie Base is Saucepan Brownies (see index) with nuts omitted.

Heat oven to 325 degrees. Line a 9" round cake pan with foil; lightly and gently grease foil.

For the Brownie Base: Melt the butter and chocolate in a medium saucepan over low heat, stirring constantly. Remove saucepan from heat; cool slightly.

With a large spoon, blend in sugar and vanilla. Blend in eggs. Stir in flour, baking powder, and salt until blended. Spread into prepared pan. Bake for 20 to 25 minutes or until a cake tester or toothpick inserted near the center comes out with a few moist crumbs attached. Cool pan completely on a wire rack. Then remove Brownie Base from pan and gently remove foil.

For the Topping: Gently heat cream and caramel sauce of your choice in a small saucepan over low heat, stirring often until well blended and pourable. Drizzle over Brownie Base, then immediately sprinkle with white chocolate. Cool completely to allow mixture to set up. Cut into wedges. Makes about 10.

Walnut Fudge Brownie with Ganache and Caramel Sauce

This is a terrific, easy-to-make dessert with those extra-special touches that make it perfect for entertaining (either yourself or others!). I like to serve it with an assortment of fresh berries or sliced peaches on the individual plates. It always "wows" them in my chocolate classes!

BROWNIE BASE
Cocoa powder, sifted, for coating pan
1 cup unsalted butter, softened to
    room temperature
1¾ cups granulated sugar
⅔ cup brown rice syrup
3 large eggs, lightly beaten
1¾ cups unbleached, all-purpose flour
¾ cup unsweetened cocoa powder,
    sifted
½ tsp. salt
¼ cup milk, whole or 2 percent
2 cups coarsely chopped walnuts,
    toasted

GANACHE
1 cup heavy (whipping) cream
6 or 7 oz. semisweet chocolate, finely
    chopped

SAUCE
In a Hurry Caramel Sauce (see index)

Heat oven to 325 degrees. Lightly grease a 10" springform pan, then coat with a few sprinkles cocoa powder, tapping out excess.

For the Brownie Base: In a large bowl of an electric mixer, beat the butter and sugar on medium-high speed until light and fluffy. Blend in syrup on medium speed. Add eggs, mixing gently to blend well.

With mixer on low, beat in flour, cocoa powder, and salt alternately with milk, stopping occasionally to scrape bowl and paddle. Stir in nuts.

Spread into prepared pan. Bake for 35 to 45 minutes or until a cake tester or toothpick inserted near the edge comes out with a few moist crumbs attached. Cool pan completely on a wire rack.

For the Ganache: Bring cream to a simmer in a medium saucepan. Remove from heat and add chocolate. Let sit, undisturbed, for 5 minutes; then stir until chocolate is melted and mixture is smooth. Cool completely.

Gently remove ring from springform pan. Place Brownie Base atop a wire rack set over waxed paper. Pour all the Ganache slowly over top of Brownie Base; spread with a metal or other spatula to cover top and sides of Brownie Base. Let stand about 1 hour or until set.

For the Sauce: Serve brownie with caramel sauce (and whipped cream, if desired). Makes about 10 servings.

Double Fudge Brownies

I love the way unsweetened and bittersweet chocolate offset the sweetness of the cream-cheese filling in these moist, fudgy brownies.

BROWNIE BASE

4 oz. unsweetened chocolate, coarsely chopped

²⁄₃ cup unsalted butter

2 cups granulated sugar

4 large eggs, lightly beaten

1 tsp. pure vanilla extract

1¼ cups unbleached, all-purpose flour

1 tsp. baking powder

1 tsp. salt

5 oz. bittersweet chocolate, coarsely chopped

FILLING

3 tbsp. unsalted butter, softened to room temperature

4 oz. cream cheese, softened to room temperature

¼ cup granulated sugar

1 extra large egg, lightly beaten

1 tbsp. + 1 tsp. unbleached, all-purpose flour

½ tsp. pure vanilla extract

Heat oven to 350 degrees. Lightly grease a 13x9" baking pan.

For the Brownie Base: Melt the chocolate and butter in a medium saucepan over low heat, stirring to blend. Remove saucepan from heat. With an electric mixer, beat in sugar, eggs, and vanilla on medium-high speed until mixture is thick and well blended.

Blend in flour, baking powder, and salt. Stir in chocolate pieces. Spread *half* the Brownie Base into prepared pan.

For the Filling: In a medium bowl with an electric mixer, beat ingredients together until smooth, stopping occasionally to scrape bowl.

Spread Filling over Brownie Base in pan. Top with remaining half of Brownie Base, smoothing gently and carefully. Bake for 35 to 40 minutes or until a cake tester or toothpick comes out with a few moist crumbs attached, testing 1" from the edge of the pan. Cool pan completely on a wire rack. Cut into bars. Makes about 2½ dozen.

BEV'S BITE ——————

My Brownie Base is Plain and Simple Fudgy Brownies (see index) with omissions and additions.

Honey of a Brownie

Honey gives these brownies a richness all their own. They always create a "buzz" wherever I take them!

BROWNIE BASE

⅓ cup unsalted butter, softened to
    room temperature
½ cup granulated sugar
1 tsp. pure vanilla extract
⅓ cup honey (clover, orange blossom,
    or tupelo preferred)
2 large eggs, lightly beaten
½ cup unbleached, all-purpose flour
⅓ cup unsweetened cocoa powder,
    sifted
¼ tsp. baking soda
¼ tsp. salt

Heat oven to 350 degrees. Lightly grease a 9" square pan.

For the Brownie Base: In a large bowl with an electric mixer, beat the butter, sugar, vanilla, and honey at medium-high speed, stopping and scraping the bowl often, until light and fluffy. On low speed, add eggs, mixing until well blended.

Add flour, cocoa, baking soda, and salt, beating on low speed just until mixture is combined. Spread into prepared pan. Bake for 25 to 30 minutes or until a cake tester or toothpick inserted near the center of the pan comes out with a few moist crumbs attached. Cool pan completely on a wire rack. Cut into squares. Makes 2 dozen.

BEV'S BITE —————————
Drizzle with extra honey before serving.

Mint Chocolate Brownie in the Round

Not necessarily a chocolate and mint lover, I couldn't resist ordering this for dessert at a restaurant in upstate New York years ago. It was great, and it has stuck in my memory ever since. I've recreated the dish many times for family and friends. Use a good-quality ice cream as an extra-special accompaniment.

BROWNIE BASE
½ cup unsalted butter, softened to room temperature
12 oz. bittersweet chocolate, coarsely chopped
1 tbsp. instant espresso powder dissolved in 6 tbsp. hot water
2 large eggs, separated
½ tsp. pure mint extract (spearmint or peppermint)
1 cup finely chopped hazelnuts, toasted
¼ tsp. cream of tartar
½ cup superfine sugar

GARNISH
Mint Chocolate Ice Cream (see index)

Heat oven to 325 degrees. Lightly grease a 9" springform pan.

For the Brownie Base: Combine the butter and chocolate in a double boiler set over simmering water. Stir often, over low heat, until mixture is melted and smooth.

Remove top of double boiler from heat, and carefully wipe bottom (so none of the moisture steams up into the chocolate mixture). Stir in dissolved espresso, egg yolks (lightly beaten), mint, and nuts.

In a medium bowl with an electric mixer, beat egg whites (room temperature) with cream of tartar until frothy. Slowly add sugar, 1 tbsp. at a time, until stiff peaks form. Gently fold egg-white mixture into chocolate mixture, a third at a time, until blended. Spread into prepared pan. Bake for 30 to 35 minutes or until a cake tester or toothpick inserted near the center comes out with a few moist crumbs attached. Cool pan completely on a wire rack. Cut into wedges.

For the Garnish: Serve with some ice cream on the side. Makes about 8.

Nibs and Nuts Brownies

In the chocolate-making process, the nibs and shells are what are separated from the cocoa bean. The nibs (which contain an average of 54 percent cocoa butter) are ground to extract cocoa butter and chocolate liquor. Here, I've used the nibs for added crunch and cocoa-butter flavor . . . different and sophisticated! See my sources chapter for where to get nibs.

BROWNIE BASE

4 oz. unsweetened chocolate, coarsely chopped
⅔ cup unsalted butter
2 cups granulated sugar
4 large eggs, lightly beaten
1 tsp. pure vanilla extract
1¼ cups unbleached, all-purpose flour
1 tsp. baking powder
1 tsp. salt
1 cup chopped walnuts, lightly toasted
¼ cup chopped cocoa nibs

Heat oven to 325 degrees. Lightly grease a 13x9" baking pan.

For the Brownie Base: Melt the chocolate and butter in a medium saucepan over low heat, stirring to blend.

Remove saucepan from heat. Whisk in sugar, eggs, and vanilla.

Stir in flour, baking powder, salt, nuts, and nibs. Spread into prepared pan. Bake for 25 minutes or until a cake tester or toothpick comes out with a few moist crumbs attached, testing 1" from the center of the pan. Brownies will be dry if overbaked! Cool pan completely on a wire rack. Cut into bars. Makes 15 to 18.

BEV'S BITES ———————

Enjoy these with a cup of espresso!

My Brownie Base is Plain and Simple Fudgy Brownies (see index), using walnuts and with cocoa nibs added.

BROWNIE PAIRINGS

*You don't have to eat this outdoors, surrounded by flowers, but somehow
a brownie with Poached Dried Cherries just tastes better that way!*

Banana Ice Cream

Banana Ice Cream with my Brownie Banana Split? Why, you'll be the envy of all your friends!

ICE CREAM BASE
⅔ cup superfine sugar
½ cup milk, whole or 2 percent
2 large egg yolks, lightly beaten
1 tbsp. + 1 tsp. fresh lemon juice
Pinch salt
1½ lb. very ripe bananas, unpeeled

For the Ice Cream Base: In a small saucepan, bring the sugar and milk to a simmer over medium heat, stirring until sugar dissolves. (This will take almost no time with superfine sugar.)

In a small bowl, gradually whisk ½ cup of the hot syrup into egg yolks. Return mixture to saucepan; stir constantly over low heat just until mixture begins to simmer and thickens slightly.

Remove pan from heat and cool for 6 minutes. Scrape yolk mixture into food processor fitted with a metal blade. Add lemon juice and salt, pulsing to combine.

Peel bananas and cut into 1"-thick slices (more or less; don't get out the ruler for this!). Add banana slices to food processor. Puree until smooth, stopping occasionally to scrape sides of bowl. Place mixture in a large bowl. Cover and refrigerate, stirring occasionally, until cold.

Freeze mixture in an ice-cream maker according to manufacturer's directions. Scrape ice cream into a container and freeze, covered, until ready to enjoy. Makes about 1½ pt.

Cinnamon Ice Cream

Homemade ice cream goes well with any of my brownies. This is a rewarding project when you're feeling ambitious and creative. And if you never feel ambitious and creative, convince someone else to make it for you!

ICE CREAM BASE
2 cups heavy (whipping) cream
2 cups milk, whole
4 cinnamon sticks or 4 tsp. ground cinnamon
8 large egg yolks
½ cup granulated sugar

For the Ice Cream Base: In a medium saucepan, bring the cream, milk, and cinnamon to a boil. Turn off heat, cover saucepan, and let mixture steep for 30 minutes. Remove cinnamon sticks, if using.

In a large bowl, whisk egg yolks and sugar until combined. Slowly whisk in 1 cup of the warm cream mixture. Return all to saucepan. Simmer, stirring, until mixture is thick and coats the back of a metal spoon. While mixture is simmering, set a medium bowl in a larger bowl of water and ice.

Remove mixture from heat. Pour into the medium bowl over the water/ice and stir occasionally until cold.

When cold, strain mixture. Freeze mixture in an ice-cream maker according to manufacturer's directions. Scrape ice cream into a large container and freeze, covered, until ready to enjoy. Makes a little more than 1 qt.

Heirloom Sour Cream Ice Cream

I have fond memories of helping churn homemade ice cream at family picnics, and this heirloom recipe is one of my favorites. The sour cream is a wonderful counterpoint for my Atomic Brownies or any one of your choosing.

ICE CREAM BASE
1¼ cups sour cream, cold
½ cup confectioners' sugar, sifted
1 tbsp. fresh lemon juice
2 tsp. pure vanilla extract
1¼ cups granulated sugar
6 large egg yolks
2 cups heavy (whipping) cream
1 cup milk, whole

For the Ice Cream Base: In a small bowl, whisk together the sour cream, confectioners' sugar, juice, and vanilla until mixture is well blended. Cover and keep refrigerated until ready to use.

In a medium bowl, whisk together granulated sugar and yolks until well blended. In a large saucepan, bring cream and milk to a simmer. Whisk half of the hot cream/milk mixture into the sugar/yolk mixture. Return all to saucepan. Over medium heat, stir until mixture thickens and coats the back of a metal spoon. Be careful not to boil.

Scrape from saucepan into a large bowl and refrigerate, stirring occasionally, until cold. Blend in sour cream mixture.

Freeze mixture in an ice-cream maker according to manufacturer's directions. Scrape ice cream into a large container and freeze, covered, until ready to enjoy. Makes about 1½ qt.

Mint Chocolate Ice Cream

In my Mint Chocolate Brownie in the Round recipe, I mention pairing the slices with quality mint ice cream. Here's a quick, easy, and flavorful alternative when quality can only be found in your kitchen!

ICE CREAM BASE
1 half-gal. vanilla ice cream, softened slightly
1 cup finely crushed hard peppermint candies
1 cup coarsely chopped bittersweet chocolate
⅛ tsp. pure peppermint extract

For the Ice Cream Base: In a large bowl with an electric mixer, beat the ingredients until well combined.

Cover and freeze until firm enough to scoop, at least 2 hours. Makes ½ gal.

White Chocolate Ice Cream

If you adore brownies paired with exceptionally rich ice cream, this definitely will make you say "ah"!

ICE CREAM BASE
1 pt. heavy (whipping) cream
½ vanilla bean, split in half lengthwise
4 large egg yolks
½ cup granulated sugar
4 oz. white chocolate, coarsely chopped

For the Ice Cream Base: In a medium saucepan, bring the cream just to a simmer.

Remove saucepan from heat. Stir in vanilla bean and set aside.

In a large bowl, whisk together egg yolks and sugar until combined. Slowly whisk 1 cup hot cream mixture into yolk mixture. Return to saucepan. Cook mixture over low heat until thick and mixture coats back of a metal spoon. While mixture is simmering, set a medium bowl in a larger bowl of water and ice.

Remove mixture from heat; add chocolate, stirring until melted and smooth. Pour into the medium bowl over the water/ice and stir occasionally until cold. Remove vanilla bean.

Freeze mixture in an ice-cream maker according to manufacturer's directions. Scrape into a large container and freeze, covered, until ready to enjoy. Makes about 1 pt.

How could something that contains sparkling water, sugar, red raspberries, and champagne not make a bright, crisp brownie pairing?!

Raspberry Champagne Sorbet

Now, this makes for one sophisticated brownie pairing. Let the celebrating begin!

SORBET BASE
¾ cup sparkling water
¾ cup superfine or granulated sugar
2½ cups fresh red raspberries
⅓ cup water
2 cups champagne, chilled

BEV'S BITE

I prefer superfine sugar for this recipe, as it dissolves quickly, easily, and completely.

For the Sorbet Base: In a small saucepan, combine the sparkling water and sugar. Bring to a boil, stirring, until sugar is dissolved. (This will take almost no time with superfine sugar.) Remove saucepan from heat; let cool to room temperature.

Pulse raspberries and water in a food processor fitted with the metal blade. Process until smooth, stopping occasionally to scrape down sides of bowl. Strain mixture and discard seeds.

In a bowl, whisk together sugar mixture, raspberry puree, and champagne. Freeze mixture in an ice-cream maker according to manufacturer's directions. Scrape sorbet into a container and freeze, covered, for at least 1 hour. Makes about 1 qt.

Chocolate Sorbetto

This is satisfyingly rich but without too much fat, so you can indulge in a scoop atop one of my classic brownies.

SORBETTO BASE

¾ cup granulated sugar
½ cup lightly packed dark brown sugar
⅔ cup unsweetened cocoa powder, sifted
2½ cups water
1 oz. bittersweet chocolate, finely chopped
1 tsp. pure vanilla extract
½ tsp. pure chocolate extract

BEV'S BITE ———————

Maybe an ice-cream maker isn't on your "must have" list. Try freezing this mixture, once cold, in a 9" square pan. Stir every hour for the first 3 hours to mix the crystals, and then freeze overnight before serving. The texture will be much grainier than if made in an ice-cream maker, but the flavor will still be there.

For the Sorbetto Base: In a medium saucepan, whisk the sugars, cocoa powder, and water to combine. Bring to a boil over medium heat, cooking and whisking until sugars are dissolved.

Reduce heat to low and allow mixture to simmer for 4 minutes. While mixture is simmering, set a medium bowl in a larger bowl of water and ice.

Remove mixture from heat; add chocolate and extracts. Whisk until mixture is well blended and smooth. Pour into the medium bowl over the water/ice and stir occasionally until cold.

Freeze mixture in an ice-cream maker according to manufacturer's directions. Makes 1 qt.

Cocoa Cream Ice

This concoction of mine is reminiscent of "fudgesicles" from my neighborhood ice-cream truck. It makes for an interesting flavor combination with any of my intensely chocolaty brownies.

ICE BASE
¾ cup superfine sugar
¼ cup unsweetened cocoa powder, sifted
1½ cups half-and-half
1½ cups milk, whole or 2 percent
1 tsp. pure vanilla extract

For the Ice Base: In a medium bowl, whisk together the sugar and cocoa powder. Whisking vigorously, blend in the half-and-half, milk, and vanilla until smooth and well combined.

Freeze mixture in an ice-cream maker according to manufacturer's directions. Scrape ice into a container and freeze, covered, until ready to enjoy. Makes about 1 pt.

Berry Frozen Yogurt

This food-processor favorite is one I've been making and serving for years. It's quick, easy, and adaptable to any berry—and any brownie—to suit your mood and the season.

YOGURT BASE
1 qt. fresh berries (such as strawberries, blueberries, or red raspberries)
½ cup superfine sugar
¼ cup fresh lemon juice
1 cup plain or vanilla yogurt
4 tbsp. milk, whole or 2 percent

For the Yogurt Base: Rinse, drain, and hull berries. If using strawberries, slice half the quart and combine them with sugar in a medium saucepan. If using other berries, just combine half the quart with sugar (no slicing needed).

Bring to a simmer, stirring, and cook until sugar has dissolved. Remove saucepan from heat and let cool slightly. Transfer mixture to food processor fitted with metal blade and add remaining whole berries.

Process to a smooth puree. Transfer mixture to a bowl, whisking in lemon juice and yogurt. Pour mixture into a 13x9" baking dish. Place dish, uncovered, in freezer and let mixture freeze solid, stirring gently and slowly to redistribute mixture (stir ingredients toward center), about every 30 minutes.

When mixture is frozen, cut into large chunks and quickly transfer to a clean food processor fitted with metal blade. Pulse mixture, adding 1 tbsp. milk at a time, just until texture looks smooth. Place in a container; cover, and freeze for 1 hour before scooping and serving with your favorite brownie. Makes about 1 pt.

Apricot Sauce

If you've never thought of apricots and chocolate together, this fruit-chocolate combo will brighten up your taste buds. This "sauce" is a trick I learned from my mom years ago . . . no cooking required!

SAUCE BASE
16-oz. can apricot halves in light syrup
⅓ cup freshly squeezed orange juice
1 tsp. finely grated lemon zest
¼ tsp. pure vanilla extract
1 tsp. granulated sugar

For the Sauce Base: Puree the apricots with their syrup in a blender until smooth. Add juice, zest, vanilla, and sugar. Blend until smooth, stopping occasionally to scrape sides of blender to ensure mixture is combined. Makes about 1½ cups.

BEV'S BITE ——————
My favorite way to use this is layered in a Brownie Parfait or as one of the sauces over the Brownie Banana Split (see index).

Berry-Orange Sauce

Grand Marnier (orange liqueur) and red raspberries make for a sophisticated flavor combination in this easy sauce.

SAUCE BASE
4 cups thawed frozen red raspberries in syrup
1 cup granulated sugar
4 tbsp. Grand Marnier

For the Sauce Base: Puree the raspberries with their syrup in a blender. Strain pureed mixture, discarding seeds.

In a small saucepan, combine berry puree and sugar. Cook, stirring often, over medium-high heat until liquid is reduced by half. Remove from heat; add Grand Marnier, stirring to blend. Allow to cool before using. Drizzle over anything chocolaty and enjoy! Makes about 1 cup.

Orange Caramel Sauce

This fruity caramel sauce is a great drizzle atop anything with white chocolate—like my Macadamia-Nut White Brownies. But don't limit yourself to just that idea!

SAUCE BASE

1½ cups superfine sugar
½ cup firmly packed light brown sugar
⅔ cup water
1 tbsp. light corn syrup or brown rice syrup
½ cup unsalted butter, cut into pieces, softened to room temperature
¼ cup fresh orange juice
1 tsp. finely grated orange zest
1 tbsp. Grand Marnier

BEV'S BITE

Don't be intimidated by the instructions. Caramel sauces are relatively easy (a process you understand only by doing), and the rewards are tasty!

For the Sauce Base: In a medium saucepan, combine the sugars and water. Bring to a boil over medium heat, stirring often. Occasionally brush down sides of pan with a wet pastry brush to dissolve sugar crystals that adhere to pan.

When mixture begins to boil, *stop stirring*. Add syrup and continue to cook over medium-high heat until mixture becomes a caramel color.

Remove saucepan from heat. Whisk in butter, adding a few pieces at a time. Once all butter has been added, whisk in juice, zest, and Grand Marnier. Blend well. Cool before using. Makes about 2 cups.

Peaches in Warm Caramel

When buying peaches, be sure they were shipped and stored at room temperature, not refrigerated. If peaches are refrigerated before they're ripe, they get mealy and lose flavor. The aroma and flavor of a fresh, juicy ripe peach is summer at its finest. I love these peaches atop my Brownie Parfait or Brownie Banana Split. Or reverse the process and scoop some Peaches in Warm Caramel in a bowl and top with a little vanilla ice cream and your favorite brownie selection crumbled on top!

PEACH BASE
3 lb. firm ripe peaches
2 tbsp. fresh lemon juice, divided
6 tbsp. unsalted butter, softened to
  room temperature
½ cup firmly packed light brown sugar
½ cup firmly packed dark brown sugar
Pinch salt
1 tbsp. pure vanilla extract
¼ tsp. cinnamon

For the Peach Base: In a large saucepan of boiling water, blanch peaches for 30 seconds. Carefully transfer to a bowl of iced water. Drain and pat dry with paper towels. Using a small, sharp knife, remove skins from peaches. Cut peaches in half, removing pits. Slice peaches and put in a medium bowl, tossing with *half* the lemon juice.

In a large skillet over medium-high heat, melt butter. Add sugars and salt and stir until blended. Add remaining lemon juice, vanilla, and cinnamon. Increase heat to high, stirring often, and cook until sugar is dissolved.

Add in peach slices, stirring to blend. Remove skillet from heat; let cool. Makes 4 to 6 servings.

Pears in Butterscotch Sauce

Imagine a dessert plate with a soft, butterscotch pear and a tantalizingly sweet brownie . . . a great way to have your fruit and your chocolate too!

PEAR BASE
½ cup firmly packed dark brown sugar
½ cup firmly packed light brown sugar
1 tbsp. light molasses (Barbados)
1½ tsp. pure vanilla extract
½ cup heavy (whipping) cream
3 tbsp. unsalted butter
4 firm ripe pears

For the Pear Base: In a large sauté pan, combine the sugars, molasses, vanilla, cream, and butter. Stir over medium heat until mixture is smooth and well blended. Bring mixture to a boil.

Boil mixture for 4 minutes, whisking constantly. Reduce heat to a simmer.

Peel, core, and cut pears into thick slices. Add pears to mixture. Simmer until pears are soft, 4 to 6 minutes. Makes about 3 servings.

BEV'S BITE ———
Leftovers? Refrigerate and have for breakfast.

Cranberry Sauce with Honey

This sauce is tart and sweet and spicy and sassy . . . perfect for pairing with my Brownie Shortcakes and ice cream in the winter months, when fresh berries aren't in season.

SAUCE BASE

1½ cups 100 percent cranberry juice
¾ cup honey (clover, orange blossom, or tupelo preferred)
1 tsp. finely grated orange zest
1 tsp. finely grated lemon zest
1 tsp. cinnamon
¼ tsp. coarse sea salt
½ tsp. freshly ground black pepper
1 tsp. finely chopped candied ginger
12 oz. fresh or frozen cranberries
½ cup dried cranberries, optional

For the Sauce Base: In a medium saucepan over medium heat, combine the juice, honey, and zests. Simmer, whisking occasionally, for 5 minutes.

Stir in cinnamon, salt, pepper, and ginger. Simmer, whisking occasionally to blend, for an additional 5 minutes.

Wash and pick over berries. Add berries and simmer until they pop and sauce is thick (this will take about 15 minutes). Remove from heat, stir in dried berries if using, and let mixture cool. Makes about 2½ cups.

Warm Cherry Sauce

How can you resist eating an abundance of fruits when we have so many varieties and flavors available? Dark red cherries are a favorite of mine, and I've always loved the way they stain every-thing—especially as a kid when I didn't have to worry about it as much. This makes for a refreshing change as one of the sauces over my Brownie Banana Split, but don't limit your creative sauce uses to just that recipe.

SAUCE BASE
1 lb. ripe, dark red cherries, pitted
¼ cup granulated sugar, divided
1 tbsp. Kirsch
½ tsp. fresh lemon juice
½ tsp. pure vanilla extract

BEV'S BITES

Stirring crushes fruit, so what's a cook to do? Shaking the saucepan vigorously moves and cooks the cherries while keeping them intact.

No Kirsch in the house? Try substituting 100 percent cherry juice or pomegranate juice for a tasty, nonalcoholic substitute.

For the Sauce Base: In a large saucepan over medium-high heat, place a single layer of the cherries. Sprinkle with *some* sugar. Cook just until sugar melts and cherries begin to release their juices.

Transfer mixture to a medium bowl. Repeat with remaining cherries, in batches, until all cherries are cooked. (Use additional sugar or less sugar as needed.)

When all cherries and their juices are in the bowl, stir in Kirsch, lemon juice, and vanilla. Makes about 1¾ cups sauce.

Chocolate Caramel Sauce

This is sensational atop Brownie Shortcakes or my Brownie Banana Split (see index). Honestly, it's great eaten out of the pan, too!

SAUCE BASE

¼ cup **In a Hurry Caramel Sauce or All the Time in the World Caramel Sauce (see index)**

½ cup **heavy (whipping) cream**

6 oz. **semisweet chocolate, coarsely chopped**

1 tbsp. **unsalted butter, softened to room temperature**

BEV'S BITE ————
Leftovers? Store, covered, in the refrigerator.

For the Sauce Base: In a small saucepan over low heat, combine the ingredients. Stir constantly until well blended and smooth. Remove saucepan from heat; set aside to cool slightly before using. Makes about 2 cups.

Smooth and Silky Fudge Sauce

From my first cookbook, No Reservations Required, *this is a favorite, quick fudge sauce that I've been making at home since the beginning of time! Quality ingredients make for an unbelievably smooth and, yes, silky fudge sauce.*

SAUCE BASE
4 oz. bittersweet chocolate, coarsely chopped
1/3 cup unsalted butter, softened to room temperature
1 1/3 cups confectioners' sugar, sifted
3/4 cup half-and-half
1 tsp. pure vanilla extract

For the Sauce Base: In a medium saucepan, combine the chocolate and butter. Let soften over low heat, stirring until mixture is almost blended.

Whisk in sugar and half-and-half. Cook, whisking, over medium heat until mixture comes to a boil. Reduce heat to low and cook, whisking often, for 5 minutes.

Remove saucepan from heat. Whisk in vanilla. Cool to room temperature and use immediately or store (well hidden), cooled and covered, in the refrigerator. Makes about 2 1/4 cups.

Velvety Smooth Fudge Sauce

This smooth sauce is not quite as sweet as my Smooth and Silky one. Try them both. They each make a spectacular finish to a brownie!

SAUCE BASE
1 1/2 cups heavy (whipping) cream
1/3 cup confectioners' sugar, sifted
2 oz. semisweet chocolate, coarsely chopped
2 oz. unsweetened chocolate, coarsely chopped
1 tsp. pure vanilla extract

For the Sauce Base: In a medium saucepan over low heat, combine the cream and sugar. Cook, whisking, until mixture boils.

Add chocolates and continue to whisk until mixture is smooth and well combined. Remove from heat. Stir in vanilla. Serve warm, room temperature, or cold. Makes about 2 cups.

BEV'S BITE ——————
As long as my husband, John, isn't around, this sauce keeps well for several weeks in a covered container in the refrigerator.

So simple to prepare, this Smooth and Silky Fudge Sauce makes a seductive topping for almost anything.

Chocolate Marshmallow Sauce

Imagine this: I Love Rocky Road! Brownies, a scoop of chocolate ice cream, and a drizzle (a big drizzle) of Chocolate Marshmallow Sauce! Stop dreaming and start baking. . . .

SAUCE BASE
4 oz. semisweet chocolate, coarsely
   chopped
1⅓ cups half-and-half
1 cup mini marshmallows

For the Sauce Base: In a medium saucepan, combine the ingredients. Cook over low heat, stirring constantly, until mixture is melted, blended, and smooth. Serve warm or cool, storing any leftovers in a covered container in the refrigerator. Makes 2 cups.

Chocolate Walnut Sauce

Now this is my kind of sauce . . . chocolate, unsalted butter, cream, and toasted walnuts. I like to serve a small square of my Atomic Brownie with a small scoop of vanilla ice cream, a drizzle of this sauce, and a few fresh strawberries on the side (if they're in season). Let your imagination be your guide.

SAUCE BASE
5 oz. bittersweet chocolate, coarsely
   chopped
1 tbsp. unsalted butter, softened to
   room temperature
¾ cup granulated sugar
¼ cup firmly packed light brown sugar
1 cup heavy (whipping) cream
1 tsp. pure vanilla extract
1 cup coarsely chopped walnuts,
   toasted

For the Sauce Base: Melt the chocolate and butter in a medium saucepan over low heat, stirring until mixture is blended and smooth.

Remove saucepan from heat. Stir in sugars and cream. Return to heat and cook, stirring often, over medium-low heat until sauce is smooth and silky and mixture is well combined.

Remove saucepan from heat. Stir in vanilla and walnuts. Makes about 2 cups.

BEV'S BITE —————
Leftovers? Store, covered, in the refrigerator for up to 2 weeks.

White Chocolate Sauce

Oh, the possibilities are endless with this sauce. And honestly, it's just another excuse for extra chocolate with any of my brownies.

SAUCE BASE
1½ cups heavy (whipping) cream
⅓ cup confectioners' sugar, sifted
5 oz. white chocolate, coarsely chopped
1 tbsp. pure vanilla extract

BEV'S BITE
Leftovers? Store, covered, in the refrigerator.

For the Sauce Base: Combine the cream and sugar in a medium saucepan, whisking until blended. Cook over medium heat, stirring constantly, until mixture boils.

Reduce heat to low and simmer for 2 minutes. Remove from heat. Quickly add chocolate and vanilla, stirring until mixture is blended and smooth. Serve warm, room temperature, or cool. Makes about 2½ cups.

Raspberry Chocolate Sauce

If you need chocolate luxury, this sauce is unsurpassed. Drizzle it on any brownie and savor the flavors.

SAUCE BASE
4 oz. unsweetened chocolate, coarsely
  chopped
⅔ cup granulated sugar
¼ cup heavy (whipping) cream
1 tbsp. unsalted butter, softened to
  room temperature
1 tsp. pure vanilla extract
2 cups fresh red raspberries

BEV'S BITE
Leftovers? Store, covered, in the refrigerator for 2 weeks.

For the Sauce Base: Melt the chocolate in a saucepan over very low heat, stirring constantly. Add sugar and cream, stirring to combine. Cook sauce on medium heat for 6 minutes, whisking often.

Remove saucepan from heat. Whisk in butter and vanilla, mixing well.

Press raspberries through a strainer with the back of a large spoon to remove seeds. Stir strained raspberries into sauce. Makes about 1½ cups.

Raspberry Coulis

Seen on more restaurant plates than parsley (and that's good, because I hate parsley with brownies!), "coulis" is a sophisticated-sounding name and taste for a very simple preparation. Raspberry coulis goes well with any classic brownie, drizzled across the plate before serving.

COULIS BASE
Two 12-oz. bags frozen red raspberries in syrup, thawed
½ cup superfine sugar
¼ cup seedless raspberry jam

For the Coulis Base: Puree the raspberries and sugar in a food processor fitted with the metal blade. Scrape down sides of bowl and pulse again to ensure a smooth, well-blended mixture. Strain through a fine sieve to remove seeds.

Transfer mixture to a small bowl. Stir in jam. Cover and refrigerate until ready to use. Makes about 2 cups.

BEV'S BITE
I know you're looking around for the rest of the directions, but that's it! Easy—and you thought seasoned cooks labored for hours on this one. Just think, the time you saved making this quick coulis gives you more time to bake brownies.

Raspberry Cream

A fluff of whipped cream all rosy with pureed sweetened red raspberries, this is sensational atop any of the following: Brownie Cake Poked with Red Raspberries, Brownie Shortcakes, Double Fudge Brownies, Snow-White Raspberry Brownies . . . and the list goes on and on!

CREAM BASE
1 cup frozen red raspberries in syrup, thawed
1½ cups heavy (whipping) cream
6 tbsp. confectioners' sugar, sifted

For the Cream Base: Puree the raspberries with their syrup in a blender. Strain pureed mixture, discarding seeds.

In a large bowl with an electric mixer, beat cream with sugar until stiff peaks form. Fold puree into cream, a third at a time. Makes about 2½ cups.

BEV'S BITE
Plan ahead. This is best used immediately after preparing. It will, however, hold up for 1 hour, covered and refrigerated.

White Chocolate Pastry Cream

This white chocolate "custard" cream pairs well with any of my simple brownies.

PASTRY CREAM BASE

2 cups heavy (whipping) cream, divided
¼ cup granulated sugar
2 tsp. cornstarch or arrowroot
2 large egg yolks
1 tsp. pure vanilla extract
4 oz. white chocolate, coarsely chopped

BEV'S BITES

Serve this pastry cream with brownie bars of your choice, either pooled at the bottom of individual plates with a brownie set atop, or layered in a dessert dish with brownie bars to make a sort of parfait.

Leftovers? Store, covered, in the refrigerator.

For the Pastry Cream Base: In a small saucepan over medium heat, bring 1 cup of the cream to a simmer. Remove saucepan from heat.

In a medium bowl with an electric mixer, beat together sugar, cornstarch/arrowroot, and egg yolks until light and creamy. Slowly add warm cream, beating continuously.

Scrape contents of bowl back into saucepan, adding in vanilla. Cook over medium heat, stirring constantly. "Custard" is ready when it becomes thick and coats back of a metal spoon. Remove from heat. Quickly stir in chocolate until melted and blended. Set aside to cool.

When ready to serve, in a small bowl with an electric mixer, beat the remaining *cold* cream at high speed until stiff peaks form. Fold whipped cream into white chocolate "custard." Makes about 2½ cups.

With this White Chocolate Cream paired with fresh-from-our-garden blueberries and slathered in a Brownie Shortcake, I question this whole concept of sharing!

White Chocolate Cream

My favorite way to serve this is layered in my Brownie Shortcakes, instead of ice cream, and topped with the freshest, sweetest seasonal berries.

CREAM BASE
1 cup milk, whole
1 vanilla bean, split in half lengthwise
3 large egg yolks
⅓ cup granulated sugar
2 tbsp. cornstarch or arrowroot
2 tbsp. unsalted butter, softened to room temperature
2 oz. white chocolate, coarsely chopped

For the Cream Base: In a medium saucepan, bring the milk and vanilla bean to a boil. Remove from heat; cover and allow to steep for 15 minutes.

In a medium bowl with an electric mixer, beat together egg yolks and sugar on medium-high speed until light and lemon colored. On low speed, blend in cornstarch/arrowroot.

Whisk about 1 cup warm milk into yolk mixture. Return to saucepan. Bring to a boil, whisking constantly and boiling for 1 minute.

Remove saucepan from heat, and carefully and quickly remove vanilla bean. Whisk in butter and white chocolate until mixture is blended and smooth. Strain the "custard" into a bowl and place a piece of plastic wrap directly on the surface of the pastry cream. Refrigerate until cold. Makes about 1½ cups.

Praline Pecan Sauce

This buttery, rich sauce drizzles well over any of my deep, dark, intense brownies.

SAUCE BASE
½ cup unsalted butter, softened to room temperature
1 cup firmly packed light brown sugar
2 tbsp. cornstarch or arrowroot
3 cups half-and-half
1 tbsp. pure vanilla extract
¾ cup coarsely chopped, toasted salted pecans

For the Sauce Base: Melt the butter in a medium saucepan over medium heat. Whisk in sugar and cornstarch/arrowroot until blended.

Whisk in half-and-half and vanilla. Cook, stirring occasionally, until sauce begins to thicken. When thick, remove from heat and stir in pecans. Set aside to cool slightly or serve immediately. Makes about 3 cups.

BEV'S BITE
Leftovers? Store, covered, in the refrigerator.

Fresh Mango "Butter"

Slather some of this atop an unfrosted, warm brownie and, well, it's maddening!

"BUTTER" BASE
5 lb. very ripe mangoes
1 cup fresh lime or orange juice
1 cup granulated sugar
2 cinnamon sticks or 2 tsp. ground
   cinnamon

BEV'S BITE
When you're breezing through the produce section and you see golden-red, very ripe mangoes on sale, snatch them up and make this recipe. It keeps, covered, in the refrigerator for 1 week or frozen for several months.

For the "Butter" Base: Peel and thickly slice the mangoes. Puree mangoes and juice in 2 or 3 batches in a food processor fitted with the metal blade. Mixture should be smooth and well combined.

In a large saucepan, combine mango puree, sugar, and cinnamon. Bring to a boil over medium heat, stirring constantly.

Reduce heat to low and simmer, stirring, until very thick. This will take about 1 hour and you need to be careful—mixture will bubble and spatter. You are looking for a final cooked consistency similar to apple butter. (Be sure to stir often. This will prevent burning and scorching.)

Remove saucepan from heat. Remove cinnamon sticks if using. Let mixture cool before using. Makes about 4 cups.

Warm Mango Compote

I can't get enough of fresh mangoes and use every excuse I can to create with them. When I was in Kenya and Tanzania, I had a variation of this compote with breakfast each morning, and I have since paired it with freshly baked brownies at my home. Warm brownies and Warm Mango Compote for breakfast, anyone?!

COMPOTE BASE
1 vanilla bean
¼ cup granulated sugar
¾ cup water
3 medium mangoes

BEV'S BITE

What to do with that scraped vanilla bean? Let it dry on paper towels. When it is completely dry, stick the bean in a small jar of granulated sugar. Now you will have flavored vanilla sugar at the ready for sprinkling on this and that and for baking.

For the Compote Base: Split the vanilla bean in half lengthwise. Scrape seeds into sugar, mixing well.

In a medium nonstick saucepan, bring seeds/sugar and water to a boil. Add scraped vanilla bean and simmer mixture for 12 minutes.

While mixture is simmering, peel and dice mangoes. Add to the syrup and simmer for 1 minute. Remove saucepan from heat and remove vanilla bean. Let mixture cool slightly and then serve. Makes about 1½ cups.

Poached Dried Cherries

I love dried cherries, and I must confess that half the fun is serving something as simple as poached dried fruit. Serve this atop one of your brownie favorites. Remember the mantra when it comes to cooking with wine . . . if it's not good enough to drink, it's not good enough to use for cooking!

CHERRY BASE
½ cup dry white wine
½ cup 100 percent tart cherry juice
½ cup superfine sugar
1 cup dried tart cherries

For the Cherry Base: In a small saucepan, bring the wine, juice, and sugar to a boil, stirring often until sugar is dissolved.

Remove saucepan from heat. Add cherries and cover. Let stand, covered, for 1 hour.

Drain cherries in a sieve. Reserve liquid for drinking. Makes about 1¼ cups poached cherries.

BROWNIES AS ART: DIPPED, DUNKED, AND LAYERED

*With all these varieties of Cutout-Shaped Brownies
(and so much more) to choose from, isn't it time
to have a brownie party?*

Brownie Bites

These are small, simple, and oh so good!

BROWNIE BASE
2 oz. semisweet chocolate, coarsely
   chopped
4 oz. bittersweet chocolate, coarsely
   chopped
½ cup unsalted butter, softened to
   room temperature
2 large eggs, lightly beaten
¾ cup firmly packed light brown sugar
1½ tsp. pure vanilla extract
¾ cup unbleached, all-purpose flour
½ tsp. baking powder
¼ tsp. salt

GANACHE
8 oz. white chocolate, finely chopped
½ cup + 1 tbsp. heavy (whipping)
   cream
Pinch salt
¼ tsp. pure vanilla extract

TOPPING
Semisweet chocolate

Heat oven to 350 degrees. Line mini muffin pans with mini muffin papers.

For the Brownie Base: Combine the chocolates and butter in a medium saucepan. Stir often over low heat until mixture is melted and smooth. Remove saucepan from heat; cool slightly.

In a large bowl with an electric mixer, beat eggs and sugar on medium-high speed until thick. On low speed, beat in vanilla and chocolate mixture until mixed. Stir in flour, baking powder, and salt. Spoon batter into muffin cups. Bake for 12 minutes or until the centers still look moist but spring back when lightly touched. Test with a cake tester or a toothpick; it should yield moist crumbs. Cool pan for 5 minutes, then remove brownies from pan and cool them completely on a wire rack.

For the Ganache: Place chocolate in a small, heatproof bowl and set aside.

Heat cream, salt, and vanilla in a small saucepan over medium heat until mixture just begins to simmer. Pour over chocolate, letting mixture sit until chocolate is softened (about 5 minutes). Stir until chocolate is completely melted and smooth. Chill for 30 minutes.

Spoon Ganache atop each Brownie Bite. Refrigerate to allow the Ganache to set. When ready to enjoy these tasty Brownie Bites, grate some semisweet chocolate atop and serve. Makes 2 dozen.

Make-Ahead Brownie Sundae

Imagine having a brownie sundae all ready in the freezer. Just decorate with fresh fruit and serve.

BROWNIE BASE
4 oz. unsweetened chocolate, coarsely
   chopped
⅔ cup unsalted butter
2 cups granulated sugar
4 large eggs, lightly beaten
1 tsp. pure vanilla extract
1¼ cups unbleached, all-purpose flour
1 tsp. baking powder
1 tsp. salt
1 cup chopped walnuts or pecans,
   lightly toasted

FILLING
1 qt. ice cream (flavor of your choice)

TOPPING
Smooth and Silky Fudge Sauce
   (see index)

Heat oven to 350 degrees. Lightly grease a 13x9" baking pan.

For the Brownie Base: Melt the chocolate and butter in a medium saucepan over low heat, stirring to blend.

Remove saucepan from heat. Whisk in sugar, eggs, and vanilla to blend.

Stir in flour, baking powder, salt, and nuts until combined. Spread into prepared pan. Bake for 25 minutes or until brownies *just* begin to pull away from sides of pan. Brownies will be dry if overbaked! Cool pan completely on a wire rack.

For the Filling: Place ice cream in refrigerator to soften for 30 minutes. Then scoop the entire quart atop the brownie layer. Return to freezer for 2 hours or until firm.

For the Topping: Pour sauce over filling; freeze. Cut into squares. Makes about 12.

BEV'S BITES —————

I love to serve each square with a dollop of freshly whipped cream, some toasted walnut pieces, and sliced fresh strawberries when they're in season or frozen strawberries, thawed, when they're not.

My Brownie Base is Plain and Simple Fudgy Brownies (see index).

Can you imagine? I filled mine with fudge swirl ice cream. Yum!

Brownie Ice-Cream Sandwiches

When I was a kid, an ice-cream sandwich was one of my favorite treats from the "ice-cream truck." Growing up in New Jersey, we had the Good Humor Ice Cream man—I was always so disappointed he didn't tell me a joke first! Now that I'm grown up (?), I love to stock these in my freezer for that brownie and ice cream fix, without the fuss!

Heat oven to 350 degrees. Lightly grease two 13x9" baking pans.

For the Brownie Base: Melt the chocolate and butter in a large saucepan over low heat, stirring to blend.

Remove saucepan from heat. Whisk in sugar, eggs, and vanilla to blend.

Stir in flour, baking powder, and salt to combine. Spread into prepared pans. Bake for 25 minutes or until brownies *just* begin to pull away from sides of pans. Brownies will be dry if over-baked! Cool pans completely on a wire rack. *Do not cut.*

For the Ice-Cream Base: Place ice cream in refrigerator to soften for 30 minutes. Then scoop the entire half-gallon atop one of the brownie layers. Gently spread ice cream evenly over the brownie. Place the second brownie layer onto the ice cream, keeping what was the top of the baked brownie up. Carefully press layers into place. Return to freezer for 1½ hours.

When ready to cut, remove from freezer and place on a large cutting board. Cut in half lengthwise, and then cut each strip crosswise into thirds. Cut each square diagonally to form 12 triangles. Serve immediately, or wrap each "sandwich" in plastic wrap and store in freezer for future enjoyment. Makes 12.

BROWNIE BASE

8 oz. unsweetened chocolate, coarsely chopped
1⅓ cups unsalted butter
4 cups granulated sugar
8 large eggs, lightly beaten
2 tsp. pure vanilla extract
2½ cups unbleached, all-purpose flour
2 tsp. baking powder
2 tsp. salt

ICE-CREAM BASE

½ gal. good-quality ice cream

BEV'S BITES

Flavor ideas for the ice cream include purchased vanilla, fudge swirl, or toffee crunch. If you're feeling ambitious, make the Mint Chocolate Ice Cream, Cinnamon Ice Cream, Heirloom Sour Cream Ice Cream, or White Chocolate Ice Cream (see index for these).

These make large triangular sandwiches. You can, of course, make other shapes and sizes.

My Brownie Base is 2 batches of Plain and Simple Fudgy Brownies (see index) with nuts omitted.

My Alaska, Brownie Style

This luscious combination of brownie, ice creams, meringue, and fudge sauce makes a simply spectacular dessert that really is not that difficult to execute.

BROWNIE BASE
½ cup unsalted butter
2 oz. unsweetened chocolate, coarsely chopped
1 cup granulated sugar
1 tsp. pure vanilla extract
2 large eggs, lightly beaten
⅔ cup unbleached, all-purpose flour
½ tsp. baking powder
¼ tsp. salt
½ cup chopped nuts, if desired (hazelnuts, pecans, walnuts, or almonds)

ICE-CREAM BASE
2 cups strawberry ice cream
2 cups mint chocolate chip ice cream
2 cups vanilla ice cream

MERINGUE BASE
3 large egg whites, room temperature
¼ tsp. salt
¼ tsp. cream of tartar
6 tbsp. superfine sugar

TOPPING
1½ cups Smooth and Silky Fudge Sauce (see index)

BEV'S BITES ————————

Soften each flavor of ice cream for 30 minutes in the refrigerator before using.

My Brownie Base is Saucepan Brownies (see index).

Heat oven to 350 degrees. Grease and lightly flour *bottom only* of an 8" square pan.

For the Brownie Base: Melt the butter and chocolate in a medium saucepan over low heat, stirring constantly. Remove from heat; cool slightly.

With a large spoon, blend in sugar and vanilla.

Blend in eggs. Stir in flour, baking powder, and salt until blended. Gently stir in nuts. Spread in prepared pan. Bake for 20 to 25 minutes or until set in the center. Cool pan completely on a wire rack. Cut Brownie Base to match the circular top of a 2-qt. bowl.

For the Ice-Cream Base: Spoon and press strawberry ice cream into the 2-qt. bowl. Freeze for 2 hours or until firm. Repeat with mint chocolate chip and vanilla ice creams. When frozen, unmold ice creams onto Brownie Base. Refreeze.

For the Meringue Base: Heat oven to 450 degrees. In the large bowl of an electric mixer, using the whisk attachment, beat egg whites, salt, and cream of tartar on medium speed until soft peaks form. Gradually add sugar, 1 tbsp. at a time, beating on high speed until stiff peaks form (tips stand straight) and sugar is almost dissolved.

Place Brownie Base on a foil-lined baking sheet. Spread meringue over entire surface of ice-cream dome, sealing bottom completely. Bake for 6 minutes or until meringue is golden brown.

For the Topping: While meringue is baking, gently rewarm Smooth and Silky Fudge Sauce in a small saucepan over medium-low heat, stirring often. Immediately transfer My Alaska to a serving plate and slice and serve with the warmed sauce. Makes about 8 slices.

Brownie Pavlova with Coffee Cream

Imagine having a dessert named after you. Pavlova is named after the Russian ballerina, Anna Pavlova. Traditionally, it consists of a crisp meringue topped with cream and fruit. I've played with my food here—and created a brownie and Pavlova combo that would make any ballerina dance the nutcracker "sweet"!

BROWNIE BASE
¼ cup unsalted butter
⅔ cup granulated sugar
¼ cup unsweetened cocoa powder, sifted
1 large egg white
½ tsp. pure vanilla extract
¾ cup unbleached, all-purpose flour
⅓ cup milk, 2 percent or skim
¼ tsp. baking powder
¼ tsp. baking soda
⅓ cup chopped pecans, toasted

PAVLOVA BASE
4 large egg whites, room temperature
1 tsp. pure vanilla extract
¼ tsp. cream of tartar
1⅓ cups superfine or granulated sugar
1 cup finely ground pecans

COFFEE CREAM
8 oz. mascarpone cheese, softened to
    room temperature
2 tbsp. coffee liqueur
1½ cups heavy (whipping) cream
⅓ cup superfine or granulated sugar

TOPPING
¼ cup coarsely chopped pecans

Heat oven to 350 degrees. Lightly grease two 8" round cake pans with straight sides, and line with parchment paper.

For the Brownie Base: Melt the butter in a medium saucepan.

Remove saucepan from heat. Whisk in sugar and cocoa powder to blend.

Blend egg white and vanilla into mixture in saucepan just until combined. Whisk in flour, milk, baking powder, and baking soda, beating until well combined. Gently stir in nuts. Spread into prepared pans. Bake just until done, beginning to check after 15 minutes. Cool pans on a wire rack for 15 minutes. Remove Brownie Bases from pans and continue to cool on wire rack.

For the Pavlova Base: Draw two 8" circles on a foil-lined cookie sheet. Heat oven to 325 degrees. In the large bowl of an electric mixer, using the whisk attachment, beat egg whites, vanilla, and cream of tartar on medium speed until soft peaks form. Gradually add sugar, 1 tbsp. at a time, beating on high speed until stiff peaks form (tips stand straight) and sugar is almost dissolved. With a large rubber spatula, gently fold in nuts.

Spread *half* the egg-white mixture over your circles. Bake for 30 minutes. Turn oven off and allow meringues to dry in closed oven for 1 hour.

For the Coffee Cream: In a medium bowl with an electric mixer, beat mascarpone and liqueur until light and fluffy; set aside. In a large bowl with an electric mixer, beat cream with sugar, adding a little sugar at a time, until soft peaks form. Fold in mascarpone mixture.

On a large, round serving plate, place 1 Brownie Base. Spread with one-fourth of the Coffee Cream. Carefully peel Pavlova Bases from foil. Top Coffee Cream layer with 1 Pavlova Base. Spread with the second fourth (ha! made you think, but that's the best way to describe what's left—you're using a third of what's left!) of the Coffee Cream. Repeat with remaining Brownie Base and Pavlova Base, ending with Coffee Cream on top.

For the Topping: Sprinkle with nuts. Cover loosely and chill for at least 2 hours (up to 12 hours). Sorry about this, but it makes for much better flavor and texture. Cut with a sharp thin-bladed knife and serve. Makes about 12.

Brownie Roulade with Toffee-Cream Filling

Remember that old-fashioned jellyroll? My brownie version will keep you from ever thinking jelly again!

BROWNIE BASE
6 large eggs, separated
1/3 cup superfine sugar
3/4 cup granulated sugar
3/4 cup unbleached, all-purpose flour
1 tsp. baking powder
1/4 tsp. salt
1/2 cup unsweetened cocoa powder, sifted
Confectioners' sugar or additional cocoa powder

TOFFEE-CREAM FILLING
2 tbsp. pure vanilla extract
1 tbsp. water
1 tsp. unflavored gelatin
1 cup heavy (whipping) cream
4 tbsp. firmly packed light brown sugar
8 oz. chocolate toffee candy, finely chopped

BEV'S BITES
You can make 2 individual roulades with filling, or combine the 2 rolls for 1 thicker roulade with more spirals (as directed).

There are many ways to top this off. Simply dust with confectioners' sugar or cocoa powder. Drizzle with a chocolate glaze (see Glazed Brownie Triangles). Frost with White Chocolate Buttercream (see index).

Heat oven to 375 degrees. Lightly grease two 15x10x1" baking pans. Line with parchment paper, then lightly grease parchment.

For the Brownie Base: In the large bowl of an electric mixer, using the whisk attachment, beat the egg whites on high speed until soft peaks form. Gradually add superfine sugar, 1 tbsp. at a time, beating on high speed until stiff peaks form (tips stand straight).

In another large bowl with an electric mixer, beat egg yolks and granulated sugar on high speed until thick and lemon colored (3 to 4 minutes). On low speed, add flour, baking powder, salt, and cocoa powder, beating until well combined.

Fold egg-white mixture into egg-yolk mixture with a wire whisk, one third at a time, being careful not to overmix and deflate whites. Spread into prepared pans. Bake for 10 minutes or until tops of cakes spring back when lightly touched.

Sprinkle confectioners' sugar or cocoa powder on 2 clean dish-towels (not terrycloth). Remove cakes from oven and carefully and immediately invert cakes onto towels. Carefully peel parchment paper from cakes. Evenly trim off any crisp edges. Starting at narrow end of each cake roll, roll *with towels* (just like a jellyroll). Place rolled cakes (seam ends down) on a wire rack to cool completely (at least 30 minutes).

For the Toffee-Cream Filling: Place vanilla and water in a small saucepan and sprinkle gelatin over top. Let stand for 10 minutes to allow gelatin to soften. Stir over low heat until gelatin dissolves.

In a large bowl with an electric mixer, beat cream with sugar on medium-high speed until stiff peaks form. Beat in gelatin mixture. Fold in toffee.

Unroll 1 cooled cake; spread with half the Toffee-Cream Filling. Starting at same narrow end as before, roll cake *without* towel.

Unroll second cake; spread with remaining Toffee-Cream Filling. Place rolled cake on top of unrolled cake, matching edge widths, and roll together to make the roulade. You'll have beautiful, thin layers when you slice the cake. Makes about 12 slices.

Glazed Brownie Triangles

Take a simply delicious brownie, cut into triangles, add a chocolate glaze, place on individual plates on spoonfuls of White Chocolate Pastry Cream, and—voila!—edible art.

BROWNIE BASE
4 oz. unsweetened chocolate, coarsely
  chopped
⅔ cup unsalted butter
2 cups granulated sugar
4 large eggs, lightly beaten
1 tsp. pure vanilla extract
1¼ cups unbleached, all-purpose flour
1 tsp. baking powder
1 tsp. salt
1 cup chopped walnuts or pecans,
  lightly toasted

GLAZE
3 oz. semisweet chocolate, coarsely
  chopped
3 oz. bittersweet chocolate, coarsely
  chopped
3 tbsp. unsalted butter
1 tbsp. instant espresso powder,
  dissolved in 2 tbsp. hot milk
2 tsp. light corn syrup or brown rice
  syrup
1½ tsp. pure vanilla extract

SAUCE
White Chocolate Pastry Cream
  (see index)

Heat oven to 350 degrees. Lightly grease a 13x9" baking pan.

For the Brownie Base: Melt the chocolate and butter in a medium saucepan over low heat, stirring to blend.

Remove saucepan from heat. Whisk in sugar, eggs, and vanilla to blend.

Stir in flour, baking powder, salt, and nuts. Spread into prepared pan. Bake for 25 minutes or until brownies *just* begin to pull away from sides of pan. Brownies will be dry if overbaked! Cool pan completely on a wire rack.

For the Glaze: Combine chocolates, butter, dissolved espresso, and syrup in medium saucepan. Stir, over low heat, until mixture is melted and smooth. Stir in vanilla.

Place a wire rack over a cookie sheet lined with waxed paper. Cut Brownie Base in half lengthwise, and then cut each strip crosswise into thirds. Cut each square diagonally to form 12 triangles. Set triangles on wire rack. Spoon a few teaspoons Glaze over each brownie, spreading gently with a small spatula. Let Glaze set slightly on brownies.

For the Sauce: Place a few tablespoons pastry cream on each dessert plate. Place 1 Glazed Brownie Triangle in center of each plate. Decorate each with an edible flower if desired and available (violets are stunning!). Makes 12.

BEV'S BITE ————————————
My Brownie Base is Plain and Simple Fudgy Brownies (see index).

Cutout-Shaped Brownies

These are very simple and so much fun. Let your cookie cutters and your imagination be your guide. These are fun to serve at a kid's party—and easier to make than cutout cookies. See the index for the frosting recipes.

BROWNIE BASE
4 oz. unsweetened chocolate, coarsely chopped
⅔ cup unsalted butter
2 cups granulated sugar
4 large eggs, lightly beaten
1 tsp. pure vanilla extract
1¼ cups unbleached, all-purpose flour
1 tsp. baking powder
1 tsp. salt

FROSTING OPTIONS
Milk Chocolate Frosting
White Chocolate Buttercream
Three-Chocolates Fudge Frosting

BEV'S BITE ————
My Brownie Base is Plain and Simple Fudgy Brownies (see index) with nuts omitted.

Heat oven to 350 degrees. Lightly grease a 13x9" baking pan.

For the Brownie Base: Melt the chocolate and butter in a medium saucepan over low heat, stirring to blend.

Remove saucepan from heat. Whisk in sugar, eggs, and vanilla to blend.

Stir in flour, baking powder, and salt to combine. Spread into prepared pan. Bake for 25 minutes or until brownies *just* begin to pull away from sides of pan. Brownies will be dry if overbaked! Cool pan completely on a wire rack. Freeze Brownie Base.

For the Frosting: Cut into shapes using assorted cookie cutters. Make 1 batch of any or all Frostings and decorate cutouts. Makes about 2 dozen.

Take a favorite basic brownie recipe and your collection of cookie cutters, some food-colored frostings, and have fun! (Licking your fingers is optional.)

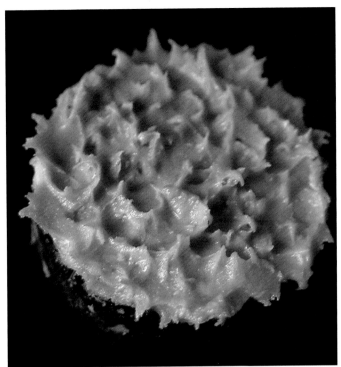

Thin Layers of Rich Brownie Filled and Topped with Ganache

Intense and chocolaty . . . wow! I love to make these for a dinner party (and honestly, I'm always hopeful for leftovers).

BROWNIE BASE
6 oz. unsweetened chocolate, coarsely chopped
1 cup unsalted butter
3 cups granulated sugar
6 large eggs, lightly beaten
1½ tsp. pure vanilla extract
1¾ cups unbleached, all-purpose flour
1 tsp. baking powder
1 tsp. salt
1½ cups finely chopped pecans, lightly toasted

GANACHE
8 oz. bittersweet chocolate, finely chopped
1 cup heavy (whipping) cream
2 tbsp. unsalted butter
2 tbsp. granulated sugar
Pinch salt
1 tsp. pure vanilla extract

BEV'S BITE ————
These are best served at room temperature, but I'm sure a few will wind up being eaten cold!

Heat oven to 325 degrees. Line a 15x10x1" baking pan with foil.

For the Brownie Base: Melt the chocolate and butter in a large saucepan over low heat, stirring to blend.

Remove saucepan from heat. Whisk in sugar, eggs, and vanilla to blend.

Stir in flour, baking powder, salt, and nuts to combine. Spread into prepared pan. Bake for 25 minutes or until a cake tester or toothpick inserted near the center comes out with a few moist crumbs attached. Brownies will be dry if overbaked! Cool pan completely on a wire rack.

For the Ganache: Place chocolate in a medium mixing bowl.

Heat cream, butter, sugar, salt, and vanilla in a small saucepan over low heat, whisking until butter is melted and mixture is combined. Pour over chocolate, letting mixture sit until chocolate is softened (about 5 minutes). Stir until chocolate is completely melted and smooth. Chill for 30 minutes.

Cut Brownie Base in half crosswise. Trim edges if dried and eat immediately. Spread half the Ganache over 1 brownie half; top with other brownie half. Spread with remaining Ganache. Refrigerate for 30 minutes (uncovered). Cut into squares or bars. Makes about 2½ dozen.

Things Aren't Always in Black and White Brownies

This is just a pretty, artful brownie with great taste.

BROWNIE BASE
¼ cup unsalted butter
⅔ cup granulated sugar
¼ cup unsweetened cocoa powder, sifted
1 large egg white
½ tsp. pure vanilla extract
¾ cup unbleached, all-purpose flour
⅓ cup milk, 2 percent or skim
¼ tsp. baking powder
¼ tsp. baking soda
⅓ cup chopped almonds

TOPPING
½ cup sour cream, room temperature
4 oz. cream cheese, softened to room temperature
½ cup granulated sugar
2 tbsp. unsalted butter, softened to room temperature
2 large eggs, lightly beaten
2 tbsp. milk, whole or 2 percent
1 tbsp. unbleached, all-purpose flour
1 tsp. pure vanilla extract
4½ oz. bittersweet chocolate, coarsely chopped

Heat oven to 350 degrees. Lightly grease a 9" square pan.

For the Brownie Base: Melt the butter in a medium saucepan.

Remove from heat. Whisk in sugar and cocoa powder until combined. Blend in egg white and vanilla just until mixture is combined.

Whisk in flour, milk, baking powder, and baking soda, beating until well combined. Gently stir in almonds. Spread into prepared pan.

For the Topping: In a large bowl with an electric mixer, beat sour cream, cream cheese, sugar, and butter on medium-high speed until mixture is light and fluffy, stopping and scraping the bowl often.

On medium speed, blend in eggs, milk, flour, and vanilla. Beat well to blend. Gently stir in chocolate. Spread over Brownie Base. Bake for 30 to 40 minutes. Cool pan completely on a wire rack. Cut into squares. Makes about 12.

FROSTINGS AND GLAZES

*A Colossal Brownie topped with Peanut Butter Frosting,
resting on the trunk of a peanut tree? (Of course not—
peanuts don't grow on trees!)*

Caramel Frosting

A friend of mine liked to use this atop soft cookies, until one day I introduced her to my version—atop brownies. She's never been the same.

FROSTING
⅓ cup unsalted butter, softened to room temperature
¼ cup firmly packed dark brown sugar
½ cup firmly packed light brown sugar
3 tbsp. or more half-and-half
¼ tsp. salt
1 tsp. pure vanilla extract
2 cups confectioners' sugar, sifted

BEV'S BITE —————
I like to use this Caramel Frosting on my brownie squares, then let the frosting firm up for awhile before indulging.

For the Frosting: Combine the butter and sugars in a small saucepan. Stir over low heat until butter is melted and sugars are combined. Bring to a boil over high heat. Reduce to a simmer and cook, stirring constantly, for 3 minutes.

Carefully add the half-and-half, and return the mixture to a boil, stirring. Remove saucepan from heat; place in a medium mixing bowl to cool.

When cool, with an electric mixer, beat in salt, vanilla, and confectioners' sugar, adding sugar a little at a time. Beat until smooth and a spreadable consistency.

Penuche Frosting

Penuche fudge is a favorite of my husband, John's—and frosting is so much easier to make! Enjoy this caramel-flavored frosting atop any of my anything-but-plain classic brownies. Just like fudge, this frosting firms up quickly, so don't delay the spreading.

FROSTING
½ cup unsalted butter, softened to room temperature
1 cup firmly packed light brown sugar
¼ cup or more milk, whole or 2 percent
3½ cups confectioners' sugar, sifted

For the Frosting: Melt the butter in a medium saucepan.

Stir in brown sugar to combine. Cook mixture until sugar is dissolved and mixture is smooth.

Remove saucepan from heat. Whisk in milk, beating vigorously until smooth. Add confectioners' sugar, whisking or beating with an electric mixer until frosting is spreadable (adding milk if needed). Spread immediately on Brownie Base of your choice.

Chocolate Icing

This is another version of a chocolate ganache—cooked, then strained to eliminate any imperfections and produce a satiny-smooth finish.

ICING

8 oz. bittersweet chocolate, coarsely chopped

1½ tbsp. unsalted butter, softened to room temperature

¾ cup heavy (whipping) cream

1 tbsp. granulated sugar

For the Icing: Combine the chocolate and butter in a medium saucepan. Stir often, over low heat, until mixture is melted and smooth. Remove saucepan from heat; cool slightly.

Beat in cream and sugar with an electric mixer until mixture is smooth. Strain through a sieve into a mixing bowl.

Let cool for 15 minutes, then cover and refrigerate for 2 hours before using.

BEV'S BITE ———

Don't have the time (or the patience) to wait? Make this a day ahead, cover, and refrigerate. Just bring it back to room temperature before using for your brownies.

Milk Chocolate Frosting

I love the comfort-food taste of this sweet chocolate frosting.

FROSTING

6 oz. milk chocolate, coarsely chopped

3 tbsp. unsalted butter, softened to room temperature

¼ tsp. salt

1¼ cups confectioners' sugar, sifted

1 tsp. pure vanilla extract

2 tbsp. or more milk, whole or 2 percent

For the Frosting: Combine the chocolate and butter in a double boiler set over simmering water. Stir often, over low heat, until mixture is melted and smooth.

Remove top of double boiler from heat, and carefully wipe bottom (so none of the moisture steams up into the chocolate mixture). Transfer the chocolate mixture to a large bowl.

With an electric mixer, beat in salt, sugar, and vanilla. Add milk and beat until mixture is smooth, fluffy, and spreadable.

Three-Chocolates Fudge Frosting

You'll love the chocolate flavors of this very spreadable and very fudgy frosting.

FROSTING
- 3 oz. bittersweet chocolate, finely chopped
- 3 oz. semisweet chocolate, finely chopped
- 3 oz. milk chocolate, finely chopped
- 1 cup heavy (whipping) cream
- 2 tbsp. unsalted butter, softened to room temperature
- 1 tsp. pure vanilla extract

For the Frosting: Combine the chocolates in a large mixing bowl.

In a medium saucepan, bring cream and butter to a simmer (stirring to melt butter). Remove saucepan from heat. Pour hot mixture over chocolate. Let stand to soften chocolate (about 5 minutes). Whisk until melted.

Add vanilla to blend. Cover loosely and refrigerate, stirring occasionally, for about 2 hours or until Frosting is spreadable. Whisk to smooth before using.

Chocolate Cream-Cheese Frosting

How do I like my chocolate brownies topped? With more chocolate!

FROSTING
- 4 oz. unsweetened chocolate, coarsely chopped
- ½ cup + 2 tbsp. unsalted butter, softened to room temperature
- 4 oz. cream cheese, softened to room temperature
- ¼ tsp. salt
- 2 cups confectioners' sugar, sifted

For the Frosting: Melt the chocolate in a double boiler set over simmering water. Stir often, over low heat, until chocolate is melted and smooth.

Remove top of double boiler from heat, and carefully wipe bottom (so none of the moisture steams up into the chocolate). Set aside to cool.

In a large bowl with an electric mixer, beat butter and cream cheese on medium speed until blended and smooth. On low speed, blend in melted chocolate. Gradually add salt and sugar, beating until light, fluffy, and spreadable.

Chocolate Whipped-Cream Frosting

One of my favorite frostings is more whipped cream than anything else. This chocolate version, to be spread atop brownies, definitely fits the description.

FROSTING
3 oz. bittersweet chocolate, finely chopped
½ cup heavy (whipping) cream
1½ cups confectioners' sugar, sifted
½ cup unsalted butter, softened to room temperature
1 tsp. pure vanilla extract

For the Frosting: Combine the chocolate and cream in a double boiler set over simmering water. Stir often, over low heat, until mixture is melted and smooth.

Remove top of double boiler from heat, and carefully wipe bottom (so none of the moisture steams up into the chocolate mixture). Transfer chocolate mixture to a medium bowl. Set aside to cool for 30 minutes. Refrigerate and chill thoroughly.

In a large bowl with an electric mixer, beat sugar, butter, and vanilla until well blended. Gradually add *chilled* chocolate mixture and beat until mixture is a spreadable, fluffy, frosting consistency. Yum!

White Chocolate Buttercream

This elevates that classic buttercream recipe to the next (chocolate) level.

BUTTERCREAM
6 oz. white chocolate, coarsely chopped
¾ cup unsalted butter, softened to room temperature
¼ cup confectioners' sugar, sifted
½ tsp. pure vanilla extract
¼ tsp. salt

BEV'S BITE
Spread atop desired Brownie Base and allow to "set up" for 30 minutes in the refrigerator before cutting into bars.

For the Buttercream: Melt chocolate in a double boiler set over simmering water. Stir often, over low heat, until chocolate is melted and smooth.

Remove top of double boiler from heat, and carefully wipe bottom (so none of the moisture steams up into the chocolate); set aside to cool.

In a medium bowl with an electric mixer, beat butter, sugar, vanilla, and salt until light and fluffy. Slowly add cooled chocolate until smooth, fluffy, and spreadable.

Cinnamon Frosting

Rich, with a hint of sophistication (and can't we all use a hint of sophistication?).

FROSTING
8 oz. cream cheese, softened to room temperature
½ cup unsalted butter, softened to room temperature
2 tsp. cinnamon
½ tsp. pure vanilla extract
¼ tsp. salt
4½ cups confectioners' sugar, sifted

For the Frosting: In a large bowl with an electric mixer, beat the cream cheese, butter, cinnamon, vanilla, and salt on medium-high speed until mixture is smooth and blended.

Beat in sugar until mixture is combined and a spreadable consistency.

Espresso Glaze

When your brownies need that extra jolt, this is the perfect topper!

GLAZE
6 oz. semisweet chocolate, coarsely chopped
2 tbsp. unsalted butter, softened to room temperature
¼ tsp. instant espresso powder
1 tsp. or more milk, whole or 2 percent

For the Glaze: Melt the chocolate and butter in a small saucepan over low heat, stirring until mixture is blended and smooth. Remove from heat.

Whisk in espresso powder and enough milk to make a "drizzler" consistency.

BEV'S BITE ——————————
For best results, drizzle this glaze over a warm (not hot) Brownie Base and let cool completely to set.

Irish-Cream Frosting

It's so much more than the "luck of the Irish" when you make something this good!

FROSTING
½ cup unsalted butter, softened to
  room temperature
2 cups confectioners' sugar, sifted,
  divided
1 tbsp. Irish cream liqueur
1 tsp. pure vanilla extract
¼ tsp. salt
1 tsp. or more milk, whole or 2 percent

For the Frosting: In a medium bowl with an electric mixer, beat the butter with 1 cup sugar at medium-high speed until blended.

Add liqueur, vanilla, salt, remaining sugar, and 1 tsp. milk. Beat at medium speed until light and fluffy. Add more milk as necessary to make mixture spreadable.

Peanut Butter Frosting

Whenever I make this frosting for chocolate brownies, it elicits the "oh, I love peanut butter and chocolate—can't wait to taste it!" response.

FROSTING
1 cup peanut butter, creamy preferred
½ cup unsalted butter, softened to
  room temperature
2 cups confectioners' sugar, sifted
1 tsp. pure vanilla extract
⅛ tsp. salt
3 tbsp. or more milk, whole or 2
  percent

TOPPING
1½ cups coarsely chopped salted
  peanuts

For the Frosting: In a medium bowl with an electric mixer, beat the peanut butter and butter on medium-high speed until creamy.

Mix in sugar, vanilla, salt, and *3 tbsp.* milk, beating on medium speed until mixture is smooth and fluffy. Stop often to scrape bowl and beaters. Add more milk as desired to make mixture spreadable.

For the Topping: Spread frosting on chocolate brownie of your choice. Sprinkle with nuts.

Maple-Syrup Glaze

I adore pure maple syrup, and Ohio has some admirable producers, even though Vermont and Canada claim the prize. This glaze is sensational as a "drizzler" over the simplest of my brownie recipes. Don't even think about using imitation syrup!

GLAZE
½ **cup unsalted butter, softened to room temperature**
¼ **cup pure maple syrup**
¼ **cup heavy (whipping) cream**
¾ **cup confectioners' sugar, sifted**

For the Glaze: Combine the butter, syrup, and cream in a small saucepan. Cook, whisking often, over medium-low heat until mixture is combined and butter is melted.

Remove saucepan from heat. Whisk in sugar until mixture is smooth. Cool until thickened (about 30 minutes).

*Snatch up pure maple syrup from a local producer and enjoy
this "change of pace" glaze, drizzled atop a brownie.*

Orange Brownie Frosting

Tangy, sweet, and refreshing best describe this fruity frosting.

FROSTING

2 cups confectioners' sugar, sifted
2 tbsp. unsalted butter, softened to
   room temperature
1 tsp. finely grated orange zest
3 tbsp. or more orange juice concentrate,
   thawed

*Freshly grated orange zest adds the
perfect tang to this brownie frosting.*

For the Frosting: In a large bowl with an electric mixer, beat the sugar, butter, zest, and *3 tbsp.* juice on medium speed until smooth, stopping and scraping the bowl often.

Continue beating until mixture is smooth and of spreading consistency, adding more juice if necessary.

Thanks for holding that Chunky Brownie for me.

INGREDIENT PREFERENCES AND SOURCES

You've already read about my chocolate preferences. I'm very particular about my ingredients when I bake and cook and, of course, have my personal favorites. I do frequently get asked to list what brands I use, so that my culinary students can replicate what I'm concocting in their own kitchens. Following is a list of my ingredient preferences for your use.

Bob's Red Mill: This Northwest flourmill uses century-old stone-grinding equipment to freshly mill whole-grain products. Their diverse and extensive product line is available in natural or organic versions. My personal favorites are: Unbleached (Organic) White Flour, White Whole Wheat Flour, Baking Powder, Baking Soda, Yeast, Cornmeal, and the list goes on and on. Visit them at www.bobsredmill.com or call 800-349-2173.

Lundberg Family Farms: This family-owned rice farm has been producing a variety of rices and rice-derived products since 1937, including their Original (Organic) Brown Rice Syrup. Brown rice is cooked in pure filtered mountain water, after which time most of the water is evaporated. A naturally sweet golden syrup remains—syrup I love to use in place of corn syrup. Visit them at www.lundberg.com or call 530-882-4551.

I use many brands of sugars, but my favorite all-around sugar is Evaporated Cane Juice (Organic Sugar) by Wholesome Sweeteners, or Florida Crystals (Organic or Natural Sugar). This is a "first crystallization," minimally processed sweetener made from fresh evaporated cane juice. Traditional Domino Cane Sugar or Domino (Organic) Sugar will do nicely, also. For best quality and flavor, be sure you're using cane sugar and not the less expensive beet sugar!

For brown sugars at their finest, my favorite is Billington's. Many brown sugars are only brown on the outside. Underneath they're really just refined white sugar. Billington's brown sugars (Dark Brown Molasses or Light Brown Muscovado) are soft, moist, fine-grained sugars. The Dark Brown has a distinctive toffee flavor and the Light Brown has a creamy, fudgy flavor. Visit them at www.billingtons.co.uk or their distributor at www.wholesomesweeteners.com.

Visit your *local* kitchenware store to shop for parchment paper. When it comes to cookie sheets and other bake ware, I love Kaiser Bakeware, especially their top-of-the-line La Forme series. Made with commercial-weight steel, each piece has a nonstick finish and superb heat conductivity. Visit them at www.kaiserbakeware.com or call 800-966-3009.

For chocolate selections, visit: www.scharffenberger.com or call 800-930-

4528 for Scharffen Berger products (including cocoa nibs); www.bernard-callebaut.com for Callebaut chocolate; www.valrhona.com for Valrhona chocolate; www.guittard.com for Guittard chocolate; and www.ghirardelli.com for Ghirardelli chocolate.

Don't forget to shop at your *local* specialty stores first to see if they carry these fine products.

It's always fun to try new ingredients and tools. Try my suggestions—you should notice a difference.

BIBLIOGRAPHY

Beard, James. *James Beard's Theory & Practice of Good Cooking.* New York: Alfred A. Knopf, 1977.

Corriher, Shirley O. *Cookwise.* New York: William Morrow, 1997.

Davidson, Alan. *The Penguin Companion to Food.* New York: Penguin Putnam, 2002.

Editors of Sunset Books. *Good Cook's Handbook.* Menlo Park, Calif.: Lane, 1986.

Herbst, Sharon T. *Food Lover's Companion.* 2d ed. Hauppauge, N.Y.: Barron's Educational Series, 1995.

———. *Never Eat More Than You Can Lift, and Other Food Quotes and Quips.* New York: Broadway Books, 1997.

Riely, Elizabeth. *The Chef's Companion.* 2d ed. New York: John Wiley & Sons, 1996.

Try these shapes, styles, and colors in your own kitchen, and find out why this brownie is smiling.

INDEX